Vuillard

Vuillard

John Russell

New York Graphic Society Ltd
Greenwich, Connecticut

To Antoine Salomon

Standard Book Number 8212-0281-2

Library of Congress Catalog Card Number 71-159807

© 1971 John Russell

Contents

Foreword

This book came into being as a result of the Vuillard exhibition held late in 1971 at the Art Gallery of Ontario, Toronto, and subsequently seen at the California Palace of the Legion of Honor, San Francisco, and the Art Institute of Chicago. When the idea of the exhibition was first mooted, it was hard to believe that the work of Vuillard had gone largely ignored in North America, and in the English-speaking world generally, for over half a generation. Meanwhile his close friend and fellow Nabi, Pierre Bonnard, had spiralled to the height of fashionable fame with large-scale retrospectives at the Museum of Modern Art in New York and the Royal Academy in London; and the Nabis as a group had gained much attention through the revived interest in Art Nouveau and Symbolist art.

Bonnard certainly has a claim to contemporary interest, in that his large compositions of southern landscapes foreshadow the propensity for painterly abstraction and colour-painting that has become so much a part of today's art. But at the same time, one felt that the large decorative panels painted by Vuillard before the First World War were certainly more advanced for their time than Bonnard's works. With their broad areas of flat opaque paint, their curiously cropped compositions, distorted perspectives and unusual colour relationships which ranged from muted, close-toned harmonies to a strident and even acerbic palette that must have been startling, these panels stand as monuments to the Nabi principle that art should strive for evocative and expressive decoration rather than rest content with easel-painting – a principle that Matisse, for one, would later apply. It was our hope that a number of Vuillard's 'apartment panels' could be assembled together for this exhibition, particularly the *Interiors* ordered by Dr Vaquez in 1896, today in the Petit Palais, as well as the decorations for the Comédie des Champs-Elysées (1913), still *in situ*; but their fragility and size was against a transatlantic trip.

Vuillard was, up till the First World War, without doubt one of the most advanced and accomplished artists of his generation. A year older than Matisse, he and Bonnard had achieved recognition in Paris by the mid-1890s, while their fellow Nabis still struggled for attention. Even the works of the 1920s and 1930s, so often disparaged, prove to solidify Vuillard's earlier contribution, even if they do not advance it; and a number of later portraits and interiors admirably illustrate upper bourgeois life in the Paris of the Third Republic.

One of the tragedies of Vuillard's early *oeuvre* is that so much of it has been lost: for when the Nabis demanded walls to decorate, the actor-writer-producer Lugné-Poe responded by offering them his theatre, and much of Vuillard's early work took the form of set designs for the Théâtre de L'Œuvre, flats painted over and over for each successive production. Unluckily, these were never documented.

Another important aspect of Vuillard's work, long ignored, is his graphics. Their range of colour, composition and technical brilliance is truly remarkable, and William S. Lieberman rightly considers that some of his prints are 'landmarks in the history of modern print-making'. The exhibition assembles them almost in their entirety, for the first time in North America; and they amaze one with their spontaneity and freshness. Vuillard began doing colour lithographs around 1896 for Vollard's *L'Album des Peintres-Graveurs* and it was the dealer Vollard who ordered from him the splendid portfolio of prints, *Landscapes and Interiors*, which forms his most important contribution to print-making. Reminiscent of Redon and sometimes even of Daumier, his prints present an extraordinary richness and variety of texture, tone and line: the favoured opaque tones contrast with clear, transparent colour, bright hues are balanced against dark ones and often the blank background of the paper itself is used. Unfortunately Vuillard gave up colour lithography quite early and his last colour print, commissioned by the art historian Julius Meier-Graefe, is the *Garden in Front of the Studio*, of 1901. The dozen or so prints produced during the remaining forty-three years of his life are all black and white, equally divided between etching and lithography.

In organizing the exhibition, we also thought it important to display a number of Vuillard's Kodak snapshots, not only because they provide documents of the period but because like Degas before him, Vuillard used the camera – albeit in an amateur way – as an *aide-mémoire* and many of his photographs closely parallel compositions of paintings. Indeed, the Kodak distortions of foreshortening, of perspective and even the cropped compositions and close-ups tell us that much of what seemed 'modern' in Vuillard was derived directly from this mechanical means of notation.

In accordance with the fashion of the day, Vuillard possessed a small Kodak, with an accordion diaphragm, which lived on the sideboard in the dining-room of the apartment that he shared with his mother. Often when friends came to visit, he would set up the camera while they talked, casually focusing on some grouping which caught his eye. Then, without warning, he would shout 'One moment please', snap the picture and return to the conversation as if there had been no interruption. Happily, his photographs convey this spontaneity of method.

He used daylight developing and, after the Kodak was taken to the shop to be recharged, he would put the exposed film in a soup plate of developer, which his mother watched while she did her sewing. Then it would be hung out in the sun to dry. Like Degas, Vuillard exploited the seemingly accidental compositions caught by the lens, in his acutely observed canvases, but he never allowed the camera to 'draw' the final design; he almost always shifted or reshaped or spread out the scene.

The people who appear in the photographs have long been familiar: Félix Vallotton, Maurice Denis, Bonnard, K.-X. Roussel, who married Vuillard's sister Marie, their two children and others in the closely knit group. A favourite subject for both camera and canvas was the apple-faced Misia Natanson, posing against her flowery wallpapers, pouting at the grand piano, or caught by surprise in the eerie glow of a yellow oil-lamp. With her, often, is her first husband, Thadée Natanson. Also captured by the lens is Vuillard's mistress, the formidable Mme Hessel, who earned the name of *le dragon de Vuillard*.

Vuillard was not the kind of artist that leaves a school behind him; his role was too individual and personal to be exploited or developed by those who came later. But his unique vision of family life in its homely setting, and of the intimate scenes of every day, show us an artist of rare sensibilities who was unparalleled throughout the 1890s and the first quarter of this century.

MARIO AMAYA
Chief Curator, Art Gallery of Ontario

Introduction

This book originated with the Vuillard exhibition which I was invited, in 1968, to organize for the Art Gallery of Ontario. When I began on that task it occurred to me that no brief, comprehensive account of Vuillard in English was then available in the bookshops. Nor was there a book in any language which offered the basic texts on Vuillard: the texts which turn up in all the bibliographies but have then to be searched out in out-of-print books, complete runs of old periodicals, and exhibition-catalogues now not easy to find. Like most other English-speaking enthusiasts I had often turned to the catalogue which Andrew Carnduff Ritchie prepared for the Museum of Modern Art's Vuillard exhibition in 1953; and now that after nearly twenty years Vuillard was again to have a museum-show in America I decided to try to make the new catalogue as enduringly valuable as Mr Ritchie's has been.

The present book/catalogue or catalogue/book consists in the first place of a pictorial record, as complete as is possible in the prevailing circumstances, of what was available for the show. To this I have added a small number of major easel-paintings which were not available for the show but are fundamental to Vuillard's achievement. In the front of the book, along with my own essay and the seventeen texts by other people which follow it, I have reconstituted seven of the large decorative schemes which played a great part in Vuillard's career: none of these was available for loan, most remain in private hands, and two of them have been split up and are unlikely ever again to be seen together. It therefore seemed to me that it served a useful purpose to reassemble them. Both in this part of the book and to a lesser extent in the exhibition itself I have tried to balance the Vuillard who is familiar in the dealers' and in the salerooms – the master, that is to say, of intimism – against the Vuillard whom he himself very often cultivated: the master-craftsman who would set himself a monumental task and carry it through to the end.

The illustrations also include a selection from Vuillard's graphic work, which in the exhibition was to be represented in virtual totality; and, finally, a group of drawings and a selection from the family photographs, many of them taken by Vuillard himself, which form so lively a commentary on his milieu.

In choosing the supplementary texts, I decided in the end to restrict myself to texts which, with one exception, either were by contemporaries of Vuillard or by people who knew him well. (The exception was the extract from a pioneering estimate by the great German critic and historian Julius Meier-Graefe.) This meant forgoing one or two classic texts from recent years – above all, André Chastel's article of 1947 on Vuillard and Mallarmé – but it had the advantage of concentrating on texts which, taken together, constitute our most reliable index to Vuillard's nature.

Every large exhibition is a collective enterprise, and this particular one would not have come about without the unfailing generosity and efficiency of a great many people, both in America and in Europe. In particular Mr W. J. Withrow, Director of the Art Gallery of Ontario, and his Chief Curator, Mr Mario Amaya, were unstinting in their kindness to me, as were the officials of the two other museums – the Art Institute of Chicago and the California Palace of the Legion of Honor in San Francisco – which had agreed to take the show. We were also privileged to have the patronage of ICOM of The Hague.

Where individual paintings were concerned I was helped both in Europe and in America by people too numerous to list here: I hope I made my gratitude clear to them at the time. It would, however, be a gross injustice if I did not say how constantly and ungrudgingly I was assisted by Jacques Salomon, who from 1920 onwards was in almost daily contact with Vuillard, and by his son Antoine, who has in hand the definitive *catalogue raisonné* of the artist. Their support and their friendship were invaluable to me; no two people could know more about Vuillard or be more ready to share their knowledge with others.

The book, as a book, would not be what it is without the help of Sir Rupert Hart-Davis and Monsieur André Zavriew, who supplied me with some *rarissime* texts. More than half of the translations from the French are by Jean Stewart, and Ben Brewster helped me with a difficult passage in my introductory text.

The last phase of our preparations was severely handicapped by a seven weeks' mail-strike in England. This intervened at a time when a number of important loans were still under negotiation and it may be that for this reason we have included works which are not in the show and left out others which are a part of it. I can only apologize for whatever shortcomings of this kind may come to light. And I should like, finally, to thank all those owners who agreed to share their possessions with others for so long a period of time. Vuillard's memory is well served by their forbearance.

JOHN RUSSELL

The Vocation of Edouard Vuillard

John Russell

There was no reason to suppose that Edouard Vuillard, the son of a soldier turned tax-collector, would take to painting in first youth and make an outstanding success of it. Even when he was eighteen he took it for granted that he would go into the army. 'I could think of nothing else', he said later, 'at which I could possibly distinguish myself.' Soldiering and the public service formed the background of his childhood, and the tradition of selfless discipline had been further dinned into him by a particularly strict and searching religious education: the Marist fathers were not men to be trifled with, in or out of the classroom, and Vuillard to the end of his days was conscientiousness personified.

His father had served in Africa under Faidherbe, whose dream it had been to extend the boundaries of French Africa from Senegal to the Red Sea. Vuillard senior was invalided out of the army in 1859. Returning to France at the age of forty-seven, he lost no time in marrying a cousin twenty-seven years younger than himself. Shortly afterwards he began a new career as a tax-collector in the little town of Cuiseaux in the Saône-et-Loire. He had a daughter, Marie; he had a son, Alexandre, who eventually followed his father's calling and went into the army; and after nearly nine years of marriage he had a second son. Edouard Vuillard was born in Cuiseaux on 11 November 1868.

Cuiseaux is nearly three hundred miles from Paris, and during his years there Edouard Vuillard had only the most fleeting and tangential contact with art. In later life he always remembered how from time to time a distinguished old gentleman would draw up in his tilbury outside Vuillard senior's office and step inside to pay his taxes. This was Pierre Puvis de Chavannes, at that time the most famous painter in France. Even after 1877, when the family moved to Paris, Edouard Vuillard showed no particular inclination towards art: the Marist fathers were still in charge of his education, and he still assumed that he would go to the great military college of Saint-Cyr. There was nothing wayward or bohemian about Vuillard, then or later: he had a great gift of steadfast application, he had a sweet and gentle nature,

Self-portrait drawing

he was very clever indeed, and he had learned to think carefully before he opened his mouth.

Meanwhile the great difference in age between his parents had had its likely consequence. Vuillard's father had been born in the year of Napoleon's retreat from Moscow; and in 1884 he died. It was a difficult moment, but Madame Vuillard at forty-five was not too old to adapt herself to the change in her circumstances. With nothing much in the way of a pension, and nothing much in the way of an income of her own, she clearly had to shift for herself. Her family were in the textile business, with a factory in the Aisne, and she knew something about the raw materials of dressmaking. Edouard Vuillard by this time was a day-boy, with a scholarship, at the Lycée Condorcet; and his mother decided that if she set up as a dressmaker in her own home she could keep that home together and perhaps make a decent living as well.

The Lycée Condorcet was one of the two or three best schools in Paris. It was also that rarest of things, a school that people remembered with affection. It had a ferocious, unrelenting, all-demanding attitude to knowledge, and it was able to claim for itself, in each generation, pupils who would arrive as clever and promising boys and leave as young men destined to make their mark in the world. It was the kind of school at which decisive and lifelong friendships are made. Vuillard formed friendships of this kind with his future brother-in-law Ker-Xavier Roussel, the son of a well-to-do doctor; with Lugné-Poe, later to become a major force in the French theatre; and with Maurice Denis, who was not yet twenty when he said one of the most famous things ever said about painting (see below, p. 20). It was K.-X. Roussel who steered Vuillard in the direction of painting; and to the end of his days he remembered exactly when and exactly where (outside a stationer's in the Passage du Havre) he made up his mind to become a full-time painter.

He and his mother were living at that time in the rue de Miromesnil. The mechanics of Parisian dressmaking had as yet yielded hardly at all to the industrial era, and Madame Vuillard's operations were carried on in a narrow, corridor-like space squeezed in between two stories of an old-fashioned house. The dresses were cut, sewn, fitted and tried on in a companionable hubbub. The materials came in long flat bales, there were screens which served as changing-rooms, and from time to time Vuillard would put first his nose, and then his luxuriant brown beard, round one of the screens to see what was going on. What he came home to was a *mundus muliebris*, a saturated feminine world; and before long he made good use of it.

Vuillard as a young man

Vuillard did nothing lightly. When he was in his sixteenth year he underwent a religious crisis so intense that he could never bear to talk about it; and when he decided to join Roussel and set up as an apprentice-painter he did it in such a way as to reassure even his mother, who can hardly have welcomed the news at a first hearing. In 1887 he and Roussel went to day-classes in Delacroix's old studio in the Place Furstemberg, and to evening-classes at the Ecole des Gobelins; in both places Diogène Maillart, winner of the Prix de Rome and hero of the Salons, was their teacher. In the following year they moved to the Académie Julian, which had an altogether freer and more lively atmosphere; but Vuillard went on with academic studies of the most traditional kind – drawing from casts at the Cours Yvon in the rue Bonaparte, and making a brief appearance in Jean-Léon Gérôme's class at the Ecole des Beaux-Arts. He was determined to prove himself in the academics' own terms, and by 1889 he had succeeded in getting a work into the Salon, for the first and last time: a Conté crayon drawing of his maternal grandmother, Madame Michaud.

Vuillard with K.-X. Roussel (centre), and Roussel's brother Henri, 1888

It is clear from the classroom drawings which have survived, and from the still-lifes which he himself dated 1887–89, that Vuillard dedicated himself with a particular sober gravity to the study of fact: a dead rabbit, a glass of wine, an apple, the naked model on the stand – all were set down in a plain-spoken, un-showy way. There was nothing about him, at this time, of the visionary or the hothead: Maurice Denis told Jacques Salomon many years later that in the late 1880s Vuillard did not at all disdain the advice of Jean-André Rixens, the Salon gold medallist, whom he admired for his professional high finish.

Roussel, Vuillard, Romain Coolus and Félix Vallotton, c. 1896

In a characteristically unspectacular way, Vuillard is one of the great self-portraitists; and from the outset of his career he set about examining himself with just that additional inner complicity which only a self-portrait can bring forth. There is for instance a drawing which probably dates from the winter of 1888–89. The pencil brings out the grain of the paper, as it had done in Seurat's Conté crayon drawings, and it establishes a warm darkness as the basic climate of the little portrait. Much of the head sinks back into this darkness, but the clear brow, the inquiring and liquid eye, the long jutting form of the nose and the voluptuous lower lip are a complete index, already, to Vuillard's character. The young man in the drawing has one skin too few; one might suppose that he welcomes the half-light, with its possibility of withdrawal. But within a year or so Vuillard had gained in confidence, as a painter, while losing none of the almost clerical gravity of his deportment in life. The *Self-portrait*

Pierre Bonnard

in a Straw Hat has, in fact, a look of the Church in the white neck-cloth, and the hat could well have been sported by a lately ordained young pastor. The right ear does not sit very well: Vuillard is happier with the eyes, and in general with the accoutrements of the portrait, which in essence is that of a threadbare dandy with high moral principles. Other self-portraits of this period show him as plumper and more composed; the *Straw Hat* reveals more of the inward anguish which for the moment was masked by a patient regard for what had been done before in painting.

Piety is all very well, and Vuillard was one of the many very good French painters of the last hundred and fifty years who gave themselves the firmest possible grounding in the great tradition of French art. But fundamentally it was with him as it was with Delacroix, and with Monet, and with van Gogh, and with Matisse, and with Braque: he did not begin to fulfil himself completely until he had fallen in, as if by predestination, with the people among his own contemporaries who had most to give him. He loved Le Sueur, and Chardin, and Corot; but he loved them as seniors, and as people whose careers were a part of history. Where his own career was concerned, the decisive encounters were with people born within a few years of himself.

All these encounters had taken place by the time of his twenty-first birthday in November 1889. Roussel, Maurice Denis and Lugné-Poe he had known since his schooldays at the Lycée Condorcet. Paul Sérusier, Paul Ranson and Henri-Georges Ibels he met at the Académie Julian, where he also came to know someone who, like himself, had done outstandingly well at school: Pierre Bonnard. Bonnard, like Delacroix and Baudelaire before him, had been at the Lycée Louis-le-Grand in Paris. He was not a Parisian by birth – his father came from Dauphiné, his mother from Alsace – but he soon displayed, no doubt by assimilation, certain master-qualities of the born Parisian. He was nimble-witted, observant, mischievous and adaptable. In matters of the heart the true Parisian is never at a loss; in professional matters he knows that, if the brain works fast enough and the intuitions are rapid and sure, there is very little that cannot be achieved. Bonnard's father was a higher civil servant in the War Ministry, and Bonnard himself had his *licence en droit* by the time he was twenty. One can imagine him as a highly successful lawyer, adept at seeing the flaws in an opponent's case and quick to seize any psychological advantage that might present itself. ('Reactions **are the** only thing that count, in art' was a remark he made in his eightieth year.)

Bonnard soon made friends with Vuillard and Roussel,

and the friendship lasted, in each case, until death. But the indispensable moment, the flash of collective intuition which marked them for ever, can be dated to the autumn of 1888, and, more precisely, to the return of Paul Sérusier from his summer holiday in Brittany. Sérusier was a big, inflammable, open-minded man who was a year or two older than the others and had graduated quite naturally to a position of authority in the classroom of the Académie Julian. Everything combined to make him conspicuous there: his age, his size, his outgoing nature, his connections (his father directed a famous firm of scent manufacturers called Houbigant), his experience of the world, and, not least, his first-hand knowledge of what was going on in the art world outside the schools. Art schools in general were boorish places, despite the presence of one or two people of potential genius; and Maurice Denis said later of Sérusier that 'in that rather vulgar environment he stood out as a man of superior culture'.

No one has ever called Sérusier a great painter, but at a time when the schools themselves were very short of ideas he was indispensable as thinker, arguer, stimulator, mimic: as catalyst, in a word. At the beginning of the winter term in 1888–89 he returned from Brittany with the little picture which became known as the 'Talisman'. This had been painted on the lid of a cigar-box, no more than eleven inches by eight, and it represented a corner of a wood, near Pont-Aven, called the Bois d'Amour. Sérusier had painted it a week or two before under the aegis of Gauguin. 'How does that tree look to you?' Gauguin had said to him. 'It's a vivid green, isn't it? So take some green, the best green you've got on your palette. And that shadow's blue, really, isn't it? So don't be afraid – make it as blue as you can.'

Five years later, Maurice Denis described how Sérusier had passed the little picture round. 'He showed us – not without making a certain mystery of it – a cigar-box lid on which we could make out a landscape that was all out of shape and had been built up in the Synthetist manner with patches of violet, vermilion, Veronese green and other colours, all put on straight from the tube and with almost no admixture of white.'

It is worth saying that Sérusier at this time was not a friend of Gauguin. He had barely met him. He had, indeed, sought his acquaintance more out of intellectual curiosity, and to find out what sort of an animal he could be, than from a developed sympathy with what Gauguin was doing. 'Nobody was teaching us anything, at that time,' Maurice Denis wrote later, 'and the secret of Gauguin's ascendancy was that he put before us one or two very simple ideas, and

Jacques Salomon at the Louvre

Pierre Bonnard

Vuillard and Roussel in 1930

Jacques Salomon with his future wife Annette and her father K.-X. Roussel, c. 1920

that those ideas were true, and that they were just what we needed. The idea of copying nature had been like a ball and chain for our pictorial instincts. Gauguin set us free.'

It was in these circumstances that Vuillard and his friends acquired the sense of mission which caused them to become known to one another and to the world, half in mischief and half not, as the Nabis. The Hebrew word *Nabi* means 'prophet', and there was a feeling of dedicated purpose about the Nabis which made it quite a plausible name for the little group. On the other hand it is important to realize that, as often happens in groups of this sort, it was the less original minds who clung to their group status, while the livelier and more independent natures took what they needed from it and went off on their own.

Meanwhile the earliest painting which looks forward to Vuillard's maturity is probably the Museum of Modern Art's *Dinner Time*. This is a very different thing from the polite, painstaking, half-lit double portrait, *Vuillard and his Friend Varocquez*, which he had begun the year before. It has, to begin with, a dramatic, back-to-front lighting scheme which owes nothing to late nineteenth-century practice. Sam Salz, who gave this painting to the Museum, took Georges de la Tour to be its originator; Jacques Salomon looks rather to Le Sueur's *Death of St Bruno*, which Vuillard had studied in the Louvre. In any case it undoubtedly has a seventeenth-century derivation. Added to this were two things without precedent in Vuillard's work to date: the use of his family, unposed, as subject-matter, and the introduction into the painting as a whole of a highly developed comic sense.

Vuillard always loved Le Sueur, and in his *Vuillard Washing His Hands* of 1925 we can see a reproduction of Le Sueur pinned up beside the bathroom mirror. But the interest of *Dinner Time* comes from the conjunction of the seventeenth century with a subject drawn from everyday. At a time when even Bonnard was girding himself to put in for the Prix de Rome, Vuillard sidestepped mythology and broke away from the sober satisfactions of still-life. In their place he put life as he lived it: the family crowding in to make short work of the evening meal. There was nothing new about the subject; what *was* new was the truthfulness of the observation, the acceptance of confusion and asymmetry, the tolerance with which each member of the family was allowed to go his own way, the freedom with which the light scuddered this way and that. The influence of Le Sueur vied, surely, with the influence of the Japanese print in the way in which Madame Vuillard, to the left, was outlined all awry against nearly half the width of the canvas. There was an echo of martial pageantry in the way in which Vuillard's sister Marie, to the right, held the *baguette* of bread: it could be, as Jacques Salomon suggests, the pose of a young standard-bearer in a battle painting of two centuries before. It is with Vuillard's grandmother, just right of centre, that the *vis comica* enters fully into the painting. It is not that Vuillard makes fun of her, but that the contrast is delicately pointed out between the ritual gravity of French old age and the eagerness with which she heads for the trough. Each of the three ladies is sharply characterized: Madame Vuillard bent over the table in total absorption, Madame Michaud the very image of revered widowhood, Marie Vuillard erect as a soldier not yet bloodied in the field. Behind them, glimpsed rather than seen, is Vuillard himself. Even the lamp on the table is rendered with a sinuous line that reminds us how solid, for all its asymmetry, is the protective image of Madame Vuillard.

Like every other student of Vuillard, I must at this point touch on the ideas of Edouard Duranty. Duranty's essay *La Nouvelle Peinture* was a great favourite with Vuillard, and it was at Vuillard's instigation that it was reprinted in 1946. First published in 1876 on the occasion of the Second Impressionist Exhibition at Durand-Ruel's, Duranty's little book was intended primarily as a defence of Degas against the critics of the day. But a great deal of what he had to say could go, unaltered, into any study of Vuillard. When Duranty says, for instance, that 'a man's back can reveal his temperament, his age, and his social position', we can think of countless paintings and prints in which Vuillard bears this out.

Duranty's view was that there should not be a dividing line of any sort between the studio and the life that went on outside it. In particular, the artist should aim at truth to location, truth to the time of day, truth to the season, truth to that *air de famille*, that quintessential kinship, which establishes itself between a human being and his environment. Contemporary life should be the painter's subject; and contemporary life demanded contemporary methods. It was pointless to pose figures in Venetian fabrics against Flemish backgrounds and hope that something of the genius of Veronese, or of Rubens, would bless the uneasy union. People should be shown as they were: uneasy, off-centre, self-preoccupied, their bodies off-balance in the attitudes prompted by habit, or by negligence, or by the pressure of unavowed anxiety. What they had on the wall, the covers on their chairs, the fall of the light from a misplaced lamp – all these were *them*, in an authentic, uncovenanted, non-arty way.

K.-X. Roussel

Degas was just the man to bear all this out. He was a century ahead of today's playwrights in his understanding of what it means when a human being cannot communicate with others; and he knew that truth to environment was a selective and not an additive matter. He was the great poet of the yawn, and the scratch, and the uncaring slump in the chair. He knew Paris as few people have ever known it; and it was with him in mind that Duranty said that an interior on the second floor was quite different from an interior on the fourth floor, and that the golden light of Dutch interiors could not be counterfeited in Paris, since it was a matter of the light reflected from steamy canals through small-paned mullioned windows. 'In reality,' Duranty said, 'the look of things and of people has a thousand ways of defeating expectation. We are not always standing in the middle of the room, with its walls running neatly away on either side of us. Cornices do not always form up with mathematical symmetry. There is in the foreground an expanding space which we cannot always suppress. That space can be very high, and it can be very low. It can lose the ceiling, it can pick up objects on the floor, it can cut off the furniture at unexpected angles. Our line of sight is cut off at each side, as if by a frame, and whatever is sliced off by that frame is invisible to us.'

Vividly as all this applies to Degas, and steadfastly as it justified those compositional devices of Degas's which to his contemporaries looked merely arbitrary, it stands up no less well in the context of Vuillard. Vuillard also acted, all his life long, on Duranty's belief that every interior has its own character, and that it is the artist's duty to bring out that character exactly. It was through Duranty, and through Vuillard's enthusiasm for him, that the square-built cabin-like interior went out of French painting from 1890 onwards and was progressively replaced by freer and more flexible procedures.

But one could believe everything that Duranty had to say and still be no great shakes as a painter. When Vuillard made the decisive change in his activity, he was prompted in part by what he and his friends had learned from Sérusier, and in part by the formulations which Maurice Denis had drawn up as a result of it. But, there again, his work was quite unlike that of Maurice Denis. Vuillard in the 1890s was not in the least a mystical painter, as Maurice Denis was. He was not at all concerned with other-worldly states, or with the phantomatic march-past of figures ill-adapted to everyday intercourse. His subject was the human comedy as it is lived out in Paris, and he saw it as a born dramatist would see it.

He adored the theatre, he mixed a great deal with theatre people, he had theatre people for his first patrons, and he could not look at even the most humdrum scene without giving it, in his mind, a trial run for the stage. If people came to call, he watched them narrowly, as clever children watch their elders. If his mother sat mending her stockings, he noted exactly the point of maximum tension, somewhere just above the elbows. He could not see a door without wondering who would come through it, or look at a park bench without wondering who had sat on it last. He was witty, and observant, and he took nothing for granted; it came quite naturally to him to set down his experience of life in the heightened and economical way which is essential to success in the theatre. But the theatre is a collective activity, and to perfect even the strongest of innate gifts he needed the company of someone who would spur him on. He had just the right person, from the schoolroom onwards, in Lugné-Poe.

Aurélien Marie Lugné was born in Paris on 27 December 1869. Like his painter friends, he came from a prosperous and orderly background: his father spent his whole life in a bank. He added the name of Poe at the very beginning of his theatrical career, and did not at all mind if people took it to mean that he was a connection of Edgar Allan Poe. (Legend then had it that one of his forebears had established this connection after serving with La Fayette during the American War of Independence.) Lugné-Poe made the most of the Lycée Condorcet in its social aspect – when Victor Hugo died in 1885, he walked in the funeral procession with his former schoolfellow Thadée Natanson – but he did not make the most of it in an academic sense. In fact he failed his *baccalauréat* in July 1887, and in October of that year he failed his entrance examination for the Conservatoire. He had even contrived in May 1887 to get himself expelled from an amateur dramatic society; altogether, the auguries for his career were discouraging, and during the winter of 1887–88 he was glad of any jobs, however menial, that came his way. Twice a week he was part of the paid claque at the Odéon; rather less often he had a walk-on part somewhere out of town. His clothes were in rags. He was so thin that his colleagues nicknamed him *le grand tuberculeux*. And then, in October 1888, he got into the Conservatoire at the second time of asking, and on 19 October, just as Sérusier was beginning to show the 'Talisman' all over Paris, Lugné-Poe appeared for the first time on the stage of Antoine's Théâtre Libre. From then until November 1890, when he went into the army for his period of compulsory military service, Lugné-Poe took part as

fully as he could – and he was still well under twenty-one –
in the theatrical, literary and artistic life of Paris. It was he
who did as much as anyone – more than anyone, in Maurice
Denis's view – to make Gauguin's work known to a select
public. It was thanks primarily to him that Vuillard in 1890,
at the very outset of his career, was invited to design a
programme for the Théâtre Libre; he was always ready to
hawk his friends' paintings round Paris, and it was to
Lugné-Poe that Vuillard owed the acquaintance of that
great actor Coquelin *cadet*, who was one of his earliest
patrons.

Above all, Lugné-Poe was the champion of whatever
was newest and best in the theatre. And at that time the new
and the good were represented, above all, by Henrik Ibsen
and Maurice Maeterlinck. Lugné-Poe played Dr Wangel
in *The Lady from the Sea* in December 1892, and in May
1893 he played Golaud in the first performance in Paris of
Maeterlinck's *Pelléas et Mélisande*. Not only did he sustain
the most difficult role, on that historic afternoon, but he
directed the play and designed the costumes. Within a
matter of months (in October 1893, when he was still some
way short of his twenty-fourth birthday), he had his own
theatre, the Théâtre de l'Œuvre: the plays in the first season
were by Ibsen, Bjornson, Hauptmann and others; Strindberg,
Ford, Otway, Wilde, Shakespeare, Gogol and Jarry figured
in later seasons. Lugné-Poe made great theatre at a time
when great theatre was there for the making, and he never
lost his feeling for painting.

All this is worth spelling out because at the crucial moment
in his career Lugné-Poe was sharing a studio at 28 rue Pigalle
with Bonnard, Vuillard and Maurice Denis. It was in this
studio that Maurice Dennis hammered out the manifesto
which appeared as 'Définition du néo-traditionnisme' in
Art et critique in August 1890. Lugné-Poe was quite rightly
very proud in later years of having egged Denis on to write
the twenty-five numbered sections of this historic pro-
nouncement. Denis at the time was still only nineteen, and
he had barely completed two years at the Ecole des Beaux-
Arts. Anyone who compares the 'Definition' with any subsequent writings by nineteen-year-old students, whether in
France or elsewhere, is likely to emerge with a very high
opinion not only of Maurice Denis, and of the milieu in
which Vuillard was a member in the 1890s, but of the Lycée
Condorcet as a formative experience.

The 'Definition' is full of ideas current at the time and
now somewhat in disrepute. But paragraph 1 has lost none
of its force. 'Remember', it says, 'that before it is a war-
horse, a naked woman, or a trumpery anecdote, a painting

Studies for a portrait of Coquelin *cadet*

is essentially a flat surface covered with colours assembled in a certain order.'

It is important to notice that Denis did not say that *instead of* being 'a war-horse, a naked woman, or a trumpery anecdote' a painting was 'essentially a flat surface covered with colours assembled in a certain order'. There is no 'either/or' here. What Denis had in mind was not abstract painting – he told his friends in later years that he was appalled by the things that were done, ultimately, in his name – but a kind of painting which would combine the tension of dexterous flat patterning with the fullest possible realization of the given subject-matter. It was a matter of 'and', not of 'either/or'.

As had happened with Sérusier, Vuillard took note of what Denis had to say – no doubt he had heard it a hundred times over in the studio – but his built-in navigatory instinct was far too strong to allow him to be carried away by it. Writing many years later, Denis singled out lucidity, on the one hand, and vigilance on the other, as Vuillard's master-qualities. Himself no theorist, Vuillard none the less absorbed what Denis had to give him.

Among the paintings which prove this is the Altschuls' *The Dockers*. Vuillard was acquainted with Henri Edmond Cross, who went over to Divisionism in 1891; and one of the painters who showed with the Nabis at Le Barc de Boutteville's in 1891 was Léo Gausson (1860–1944). Gausson was no genius, but he had been painting on a white ground in sharply divided hues since 1886; and he must have brought into the Nabi camp a first-hand account of what Seurat was like and what he was up to. *The Dockers* has something in common with the pictures painted at Gravelines, in 1890, by Seurat: the long horizontals of water and quayside, especially, and the myriad flecks of pure colour. The broad horizontal bands stand for a terracing of space; Maurice Denis's 'flat surface' and his 'colours assembled in a certain order' are everywhere present to us. The painting is, more-over, a very early example of the wish to dictate to Nature and to produce not an imitation but an equivalent of her procedures. On the other hand it has a frankly experimental character, an overplus of doctrine as against direct observa-tion. We do not believe in it as we believe in the Seurats of 1890; and, although the painting is manifestly the work of a big artist and not of a little one, we have the feeling that not enough of Vuillard himself is coming through. Uneasy in itself, the mixture of Gauguin's Synthetism with Seurat's separated small touches of pure colour rules out too many aspects of Vuillard's individual genius.

From this same period – 1892, I would say – came two

self-portraits which at first sight are purely two-dimensional in character. The transition from dark to light, which a year or two earlier had been negotiated in delicate and precautionary style, is here marked by the most abrupt of frontiers: a jagged line which runs down from the crown of the head, across the brow, in and out of the left eye, along the promontory of the nose, and down through the beard. There is no modelling to speak of. Colour-contrasts lead directly from one extreme to the other. No one area reads, in itself, as anything but a flat patch of pure colour. In the Paris version the image is octagonal, the rearground is flecked with commas of red on a green *fond*, and the bright yellow of the hair moves without modulation into the orange of the beard. Fourteen years before the revelation of Fauve painting at the 1905 Salon d'Automne, Vuillard had dared all. If it is true that Madame Matisse, when she was posing for the *Woman with Hat* of 1905, wore a black dress and a black hat against a plain white wall, only to be transmogrified in total defiance of naturalism, the feat was no more remarkable than that accomplished by Vuillard when he moved from the *Self-portrait in a Straw Hat* to the self-portraits of 1891; and Vuillard at that time was twenty-two, whereas Matisse in 1905 was thirty-six.

But those broad uninflected areas of pure paint were not true to Vuillard's inmost nature. That nature did not really thrive on the cymbal-clash of one extreme against another, any more than on unqualified plain statement of any other kind. A painting like the famous *In Bed*, which Roussel bequeathed to the Musée National d'Art Moderne, is much closer to the quintessential Vuillard in the subtlety and refinement with which sheet, coverlet and pillows are played off against one another; an emblematic T-shape emphasizes that this is, apart from everything else, a study in equilibrium, with passages of arabesque balanced by horizontal bands at top and bottom of the canvas. Even the signature steadies the composition.

It is not easy to disentangle the chronology of Vuillard's paintings in the 1890s. He himself rarely dated his pictures, and he held on to many of the ones which we now think most audacious. As to why he did this, two distinct opinions are current. One is that he regarded them as youthful extravagances which should not be disclosed; the other, that he liked them too much to let them go. Either way round, there are not many paintings which can be dated exactly. There is evidence from articles written at the time that even those who later became enthusiasts for Vuillard were finding it difficult to see exactly what he was after. Félix Fénéon, for one, wrote in September 1891 that Vuillard's paintings in the group exhibition of that month at Saint-Germain-en-Laye were 'still indecisive, with passages of fashionable handling, half-lights of a literary sort, and once or twice a sweet colour-chord that comes off charmingly'. In November 1892 Gustave Geffroy got the point more precisely when he wrote of the third exhibition of 'Peintres impressionnistes et symbolistes' at Le Barc de Boutteville's that what the exhibitors had in common was not really anything that could be called Symbolism: it was, rather, the wish to reconcile the sinuous linear manner of Art Nouveau with a technique based on individual patches of pure colour. As to the truth of this, a look across at Vuillard's fellow-tenants at 28 rue Pigalle will settle the matter.

One of the revelations of the Maurice Denis exhibition at the Orangerie in Paris in 1970 was a tiny painting on board, no more than eight inches high, called *Patches of Sunlight on a Terrace*. Dated October 1890, this exactly parallels the terms of his manifesto published two months earlier. Pools of red and orange eddy towards one another, eroding here, backing away there, frontiered with white from time to time. A gap-toothed island of pale green fills much of the upper half of the picture. Above and around it, a bottle-green jigsaw is cut off at the edges; the right angles of the left and right upper corners are startlingly precise by contrast with the rest, where an oozy curvilinear outline can be read both as Art Nouveau decoration on a flat surface and as a precise indication of the way in which sunlight floods in and out of foliage in high summer.

In Bonnard's *The Two Dogs* of 1891 we can see, equally, with what ingenuity the young artist reconciled flat patterning and jagged outline with exact observation of the way in which individual, identifiable dogs actually play together. A year later, in *The Checkered Dress (Mme Claude Terrasse)*, Bonnard used the vertical and horizontal criss-cross of the patterned fabric to establish a severe *tempo primo* in the centre of the canvas; against this the element of linear arabesque comes across with a much heightened effect of wayward independence. Bonnard had shown since 1889, when he submitted a poster design for the France-Champagne firm, that he could divide a flat surface in a way that 'worked' both as decoration and as the expression of a specific emotional message; and there is no doubt that his questing and unprejudiced spirit added a great deal to the consortium at 28 rue Pigalle. 'I do not belong to any school,' he said in 1891; 'I simply want to do something that is personal to myself.' Nor did that 'something' draw only upon High Art for its sustenance. Bonnard in old age had cheap coloured postcards of the South of France pinned up in his studio as reminders that, as he said, 'you can find beauty in *anything*'; and when he was young and interested himself in Japanese art he did not only study that art in its museum form. He turned, on the contrary, to the cheap mass-produced images that were just about good enough, in most people's view, to wrap up parcels with. 'Those unprivileged images taught me', he said later, 'that colour could express *everything*, without having to call on modelling or relief to help it out. It became clear to me that colour, all by itself, could convey light, convey form, and convey character. Values need not be added.'

Everyone who knew Vuillard at this time agreed that although he was ready to give any new idea a run he was always his own man. He was as sensitive as anyone else to the challenging beauty of the seventeen paintings by Gauguin and the twenty-three paintings by Emile Bernard which were shown at the Café Volpini in 1889. He undoubtedly enjoyed the dinners with his colleagues at a little restaurant in the Passage Brady, which crosses the boulevard de Strasbourg at a point just north of the Théâtre Antoine. When they decided to call themselves Nabis, or prophets, and when they invented a special Nabi costume, a private language of their own, and one or two quasi-magical formulae for correspondence, Vuillard went along with all that, too, for friendship's sake. The Nabis saw themselves as people set apart: initiates, for whom the day-to-day world was something to be transcended. Edmond Schuré's *Les Grands Initiés* was one of the key books of the period, and in so far as there was such a thing as a body of common belief among the Nabis it was theosophical in tone. Nabidom embraced all religions, and all philosophical systems.

Now, Vuillard was one of the least cranky men who ever lived, and I very much doubt that he shared wholeheartedly in the wish to annex the wisdom of the East and compound it with the wisdom of the West. If it amused his friends to dress up, and to describe their homes as *ergasteria*, he would never oppose it; but when he left, in *The Lady in Blue* of 1891, a record of one such *ergasterium*, he showed his priorities in a characteristically oblique way. The scene of this delectable painting is Madame Paul Ranson's drawing-room at 25 boulevard du Montparnasse (Jacques Salomon tells us that this was once the house of Madame de Montespan). Vuillard takes a great deal of trouble with the spectacular hat and leg-of-mutton sleeves of the lady visitor in the right foreground, but when it comes to Sérusier's portrait of Ranson in Nabi costume, in the top right corner, he cuts it off at the shoulders and portrays it as no more than a chromatic splodge.

It was at the Ransons' that Vuillard and his friends watched the anti-clerical puppet plays in which Ranson delighted. It would seem unlikely, here again, that he extended more than a friendly tolerance – any more than he wished to emulate another minor Nabi, Georges Lacombe, who had his studio in Versailles decorated by Sérusier and (I quote from Charles Chassé) 'carved for his own pleasure a bed representing birth, copulation and death'.

Edouard Duranty had been almost as keen on the puppet theatre as on the paintings of Degas, and as late as 1898 Thadée Natanson reviewed a performance at the Théâtre des Pantins in the rue Ballu in which the décors were by Bonnard, Vuillard, Roussel and Alfred Jarry and the signboard by Vallotton. It was, he said, an event not to be forgotten. But the real theatre, the theatre which his friend Lugné-Poe wanted to make – that was something else altogether, and I do not think that one can over-estimate its influence on Vuillard in the 1890s.

It was in the autumn of 1890 that Vuillard made his debut in the theatrical domain, with a programme for André Antoine's Théâtre Libre. Lugné-Poe had begun his professional career in this same theatre, in November 1888, with a walk-on part in Verga's *Cavalleria Rusticana*. Later he turned against Antoine, and in his memoirs he said that the Théâtre Libre in 1888 already had 'lead in its wings'. But at the time he was delighted to listen to Antoine as he talked by the hour about the 'art theatre' of which he was, in his view, the sole possible champion. Certainly the entertainment for which Vuillard designed the programme had little of the avant-garde about it; Aurélien Scholl's *L'Amant de sa Femme: Scènes de la Vie Parisienne* did not make theatrical history, and one may even wonder whether Vuillard's programme design was quite the thing for the occasion, since it shows the rounded back and misshapen hands of a peasant bent double above what looks to be a townee's idea of bare soil.

Lugné's relations with Antoine went from bad to worse. But in March 1891 an old schoolmate from the Lycée Condorcet, Paul Percheron, came to the studio in the rue Pigalle. The conversation turned on the new Théâtre d'Art, for which the poet Paul Fort was responsible, and in particular on a benefit performance which was being put on on behalf of Verlaine and Gauguin, both of whom were in urgent need of money. 'Verlaine', Percheron wrote to Lugné, 'is one of the last of the legendary bohemians. His name is known to everyone. The public will give to him gladly, as if to some *enfant terrible*, and it will be able to flatter itself that it has done literature a good turn.'

Programme for the Théâtre Libre, 1890 (cat. 116)

The performance did not do much for Verlaine, or for Gauguin, but it did a great deal for Lugné-Poe, who made friends with Maeterlinck as a result of being given a part in the last item on the programme, Maeterlinck's *L'Intruse*. 'That's how everything began,' Lugné wrote later. 'Everything' meant an association, first, with Paul Fort and the Théâtre de l'Art; the chance to put on the first performance in Paris of Maeterlinck's *Pelléas et Mélisande*; and the foundation in 1893, under a name suggested to him by Vuillard, of Lugné's own theatre, the Théâtre de l'Œuvre. Much in all this concerns Vuillard only indirectly; but if we look closely at the scene from *Pelléas* which forms one panel of his decorations at the Comédie des Champs-Elysées we shall soon realize that Vuillard knew the play better, and felt it more, than almost anyone.

Lugné meanwhile was not so preoccupied with his own affairs as to miss a chance of helping his painter friends. When they took part, in 1891, in a group exhibition of Impressionist and Symbolist painters at Saint-Germain-en-Laye, Lugné wrote a review of the show for *Art et critique*. Forty years later, in his memoirs, he reprinted the substance of it. Dedicated to those ladies, few but discerning, who had had the intelligence to go to the show and not laugh at it, the text begins as follows:

'It is now far too late to come forward with the words of wisdom which would have subdued the boisterous incomprehension of a public which came ill-prepared and was not, in any case, educated to look at pictures. But there may still be some point in risking an exegesis, however brief and exoteric, of the works on view in the south tower of the Château de Saint-Germain. First of all, and where intensity of colour, optical mixes and pointillist practice are concerned, I must refer the reader to the specialized treatises of Chevreul, Helmholtz, Rood and Charles Henry. My most urgent task, here, is to remind the reader that there exists a place called the Musée du Louvre, and that in that place one can study the great tradition of decorative style which runs from the Assyrians to our own time. All the great masters have been a part of this tradition – the Italians, the Japanese, Delacroix, Manet, all the great men of our century, all those who were reviled in their day as the Symbolists are reviled at this moment. I should like to add that the work of Michelangelo and the work of M. Vuillard (to name one artist only) are animated by the same preoccupations, the same dedication to the dream, the same contempt for vulgar naturalism, the same love of poetic syntheses. And why not, after all? Is not the whole tradition of German idealism united against the fatuous conviction that the role of the artist is to imitate

Nature? The truth is that Art has to do with subjective states and higher realities, and with them only. Art is there to make us aware of an unknown Beauty.'

The affinity with Michelangelo would be difficult to sustain today, and even Lugné put forward his article primarily as an expression of feelings current at the time; but in other respects the text is remarkably close to our own view of Vuillard in the 1890s. 'Subjective states and higher realities' might not be our way of putting it, but we know what Lugné meant; all the more so if we remember the kind of thing that was in favour with officialdom at that time.

Anyone who writes regularly about new art will be familiar with the argument that the contemporary critic is always wrong, and that only history can decide, and so forth. But Vuillard is one of the cases (and by no means the only one) in which a contemporary critic expressed himself in terms which posterity has no need to revise. In 1891 and 1892, Vuillard took part in group exhibitions at Le Barc de Boutteville's which included works by Toulouse-Lautrec, Jules Chéret, Emile Anquetin and Lucien Pissarro, as well as his own friends; and on 28 November 1892 Gustave Geffroy wrote a review which still rings true today. Geffroy's article (reprinted in his *La Vie Artistique*, Paris 1893) is not only 'right', moreover; it reveals exactly the climate of feeling in which Vuillard launched himself into the theatre, on the one hand, and large-scale decoration, on the other. Geffroy was not a 'committed' critic; he was a man – as will be clear from the extract given here – who saw the point of everything that was good of its kind.

'The third exhibition of a group of Impressionist and Symbolist painters at Le Barc de Boutteville's is something of a free-for-all. It is difficult to step back and see any individual properly, and it is equally difficult to see anything in "the right light". But artists must show when they can and where they can, and only those who see art in terms of fashion would laugh at genuine effort or pass it over in silence. So let's go into Le Barc de Boutteville's. If there are any jokers around who presume to set up as "leaders of opinion", time will soon blow them away. If there is even a trace of constructive experiment and meaningful disquiet, that in itself has a claim on our attention. A lot of artists are involved – there are 190 items in the catalogue – and by no means all of them are working on similar lines. There are Neo-Impressionists, like MM. Charles Angrand and Lucien Pissarro; there is a gifted and violent observer of the darker side of humanity, in M. de Toulouse-Lautrec; there is a painter of landscape (Bercy and the Bastille), M. Schlaich;

there is someone one can't pin down, M. Anquetin. Chéret is there, with a *Clown*, and Willette with a dubious archangel. There's not much of the Symbolist aesthetic, either, about M. Ibels' programme for the Théâtre Libre, with its reconciliation of linear design and flat patches of colour.

'Some of the exhibitors are preoccupied with the Italian primitives, and with the Catholicism of missal and stained-glass window. But the real bond between almost all the artists in question is their ambition to reconcile the linear quality of Synthetism with the use of strongly contrasted patches of flat colour. There's nothing new in this. Precise and form-enveloping line can be found already in the art of Antiquity. We have only to think of Assyrian and Egyptian reliefs, and of Greek vase-painting, to summon up some illustrious precedents. In the Middle Ages both stained-glass windows and illuminated manuscripts made use of an exact line to circumscribe, encircle, and delimit form. Many of the Primitives, also, and Ingres. The Japanese could outline a human figure as if with a single uninterrupted line; their formula for drawing in arabesque surpasses all others in suppleness and freedom of movement. As for the *tache*, the patch of pure colour, the Japanese had it, and Ingres had it, and Manet too; with rare felicity, or rather with the most masterful command, they took the *tache* and made it take its proper place in the harmony of the picture as a whole.

'If that is the tradition which the artists at Le Barc de Boutteville's aim to follow, more or less, then they deserve all our commendation. There is delight for the eye in the way in which two of them in particular, MM. Pierre Bonnard and Edouard Vuillard, make clear their allegiance. They have the gift of nuance. They can manipulate every possible complication of line – symmetrical, asymmetrical, knotted and unknotted – in a delightfully convoluted and decorative way. That's how it is with M. Bonnard's two panels. They are painted on thick-weave cotton. The one is warm and enveloping, like a tiger-skin, the other as downy and as delicate as the plumage of a young swan. M. Vuillard's interiors, his *Reclining Woman*, his *Women Mending*, his *Luncheon*, prove him to be, once again, an intimist with a delicious sense of humour. He knows how to be both funny and sad, all at once, with a hand that is as sure as it is light. Much in these interiors is left in heavy shadow, but M. Vuillard knows how to contrast this with a patch of sparkling colour or a magical outburst of light. It is time that M. Vuillard gave us something more than these little sketches, these audacious but summary conjugations of colour and line. It is time that he gave us some major works in which all this would be concerted at a deeper level.'

Geffroy was, as will already be clear, a very good critic. But he was not the only critic to feel that Vuillard's gifts were not being fully stretched by the often quite tiny pictures which he sent for exhibition. Those tiny pictures are prized by posterity. Pressed to define 'a typical Vuillard', many enthusiasts would remember the little panels on cardboard which come up in the saleroom. But Vuillard grew up at a time when the major work was the test of manhood, and by 1892–93 people thought it was high time he set about one.

Fiacres of the 1890s

One reason for his abstention from major works was, conceivably, that nobody had commissioned one. The distinguished actor Coquelin *cadet* must be ranked as Vuillard's first collector, in that he soon racked up a collection of twenty or more of his works. But the works in question were water-colour sketches, often of barely more than postcard size. They were theatre scenes, dashed off as if in the front row of the stalls; and they have an uninhibited linear energy, combined with an element of ruthless intuition about how theatre people carry on, which makes them at once startling and irresistibly droll. Looking at them we remember that the Japanese theatre also prompted bust-portraits of a particularly vigorous and implicitly caricatural kind; the grimaces perpetuated by Toshusai Sharaku in the 1790s are strikingly near to those which Vuillard set down with such relish just a hundred years later.

Vuillard excelled, already in 1890, at the application of these same qualities to oil-paint. He was a micro-dramatist from the very outset of his career. *The Visit* (1890) is like a trial run for the Art Gallery of Ontario's later *The Widow's Visit*; measuring a mere seven inches by nine, and with a minimum of facial detail, it contrives by sheer command of stance, posture, and outline to set before us three old ladies in the middle of a particularly rewarding exchange of views. There is an absolute minimum of stage-setting: simply a flood of colour, here and there. The complete success of the little picture makes us wonder what Vuillard will do next. Will he keep for ever to the format of the miniature?

Three things worked against this, quite apart from natural ambition. Vuillard's theatrical involvements led him before long to master a completely different *facture*: that of the scene-painter, who has to work fast, on a big scale, for immediate effect. The climate of feeling among his friends was against the easel-painting and in favour of the large decoration. And he had, from 1892 onwards, commissions

Rehearsal at the Théâtre de l'Œuvre, 1903
(cat. 117)

which stretched his gifts far beyond their previous extension. All these things hung together, moreover, in ways which demonstrate all over again the advantages of going to the Lycée Condorcet at one of the great moments in its history.

Vuillard's first decorative commission came to him through his friends and former schoolfellows Alexandre and Thadée Natanson, who persuaded their cousin by marriage, Paul Desmarais, to order six panels for his house in Paris. They were to be of a frieze-like shape: each had to measure approximately twenty by forty-six inches. Vuillard painted them in oils, on canvas, and they were eventually set into the wall. Vuillard at this stage in his career had not a very large range of subject-matter, and it is not surprising that he incorporated into several of his six panels single figures, or even groups, which he had already tried out in small early canvases. Two of the panels showed his mother's workroom; and in the outdoor subjects Vuillard did not attempt to crowd the scene, but relied on his quasi-musical sense of spacing and interval to make empty spaces tell. If he brought a big dog on stage, the dog's tail formed a continuous arabesque with the dog's back and the back of the servant who caressed him. If there was a scene in a park, the rounded iron backs of the empty chairs were used as markers of empty space, while the anecdotal interest was concentrated to one side of the canvas. If one of the chair-backs happened to rhyme with the design of a dress, or the dog's tail happened to rhyme with a potted plant, that served to thicken the plot, and, coincidentally, to carry the observer laterally across a very much larger picture area than Vuillard had ever tackled before.

As it happens, Vuillard's close friend Roussel completed a set of two panels, almost identical in format with the Desmarais panels, in the same year, 1892. *The Seasons of Life* is their tentative title. If we compare them with Vuillard's panels, it becomes clear that Roussel set himself a programme of august generalities, midway between Puvis de Chavannes and early Augustus John. A grave, other-worldly distinction is the mark of Roussel's ladies, even if their dresses come from Madame Vuillard's *atelier*. They are set down in an open landscape, with no indication as to whether they live a few yards away, or have come over on a trip, or are just rehearsing a Greek play out of doors. Roussel abstracts them from their normal environment. Vuillard does just the opposite. Not one of his women is striking an attitude: every one of them is highly characterized. And where Roussel's women parcel out the space between them according to strict classical procedure, Vuillard's have a look of being all over the place. Only on lengthy examination do we realize that Vuillard has pre-planned the throw-away, conversational look of the panels with quite exceptional care.

All six of the Desmarais panels are played out on a shallow ledge in space – so much so, in fact, that we feel as we feel in the front row of the stalls when that front row is a little too near for comfort. Even the lighting has something of the footlights about it. There is nothing stagey about what Vuillard sets before us, but there is that feeling of heightened awareness which comes with the very best naturalistic acting. There is a controlled elaboration about the Desmarais panels which has nothing to do with classical composition, and yet communicates a strong sense of physical well-being, so rich is the profusion of social detail, so sharp the observation, so sunny the humour. We feel, as we feel when we see very good theatre, that nothing can go wrong with the performance, and that for once every aspect of life is perfectly under control.

And Vuillard did, of course, see a lot of very good theatre at that time. Once again, the whole affair was very much a family (or, at any rate, an old school) matter. Thadée Natanson was busy translating Ibsen's *The Lady from the Sea* (though, in point of fact, he did not finish it in time), while Vuillard was working on the Desmarais panels. Lugné-Poe played Wangel in the first French performance of the play, in December 1892, and thereafter for several years Vuillard was never out of earshot of what was going on in the avant-garde theatre.

In October 1893 Lugné's Théâtre de l'Œuvre opened its doors with *Rosmersholm*. The public knew that something unusual was afoot from the moment they picked up their programmes. 'You soon realize', one drama critic wrote, 'that a pack of disdainful innovators is at work. The programme comes with a lot of rough-and-ready handwriting all over it, and to cap it all someone has disfigured it with puerile drawings.' Vuillard was the programme-designer in question. He was also, as often as not, the scene-designer and the scene-painter as well. In fact he was saturated in the plays which were done at the Théâtre de l'Œuvre, though he does seem to have made a discriminating choice among them. Ten of his programmes survive (all are reproduced here), and only one of the plays looks like a wasted evening, in today's terms. The authors concerned are Ibsen, Strindberg, Bjornson, Hauptmann, Henri de Régnier and Maurice Beaubourg (no genius, this last, but a man very much in the painting world and the recipient of one of the most important of Seurat's few surviving letters).

Unluckily we have no idea what Vuillard's scenery looked

Programme: *The Wordless Life* (Beaubourg) 1894 (cat. 118)

Programme: *Solitary Souls* (Hauptmann) 1893 (cat. 119)

Programme for a double bill (Trarieux and Beaubourg) 1894 (cat. 120)

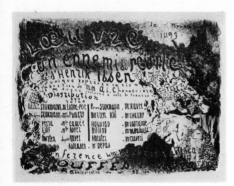

Programme: *An Enemy of the People*
(Ibsen) 1893 (cat. 121)

Programme: *The Master Builder* (Ibsen)
1894 (cat. 122)

like. The Théâtre de l'Œuvre had very little money, and
Vuillard would seem to have painted over each set of flats,
in turn, so that the next production would cost as little as
possible. There were no preliminary designs. Vuillard just
went to the theatre and got down to work. Nothing remains
of it all, and there are no eye-witness accounts, except that
Alfred Jarry did once describe, in *L'Art littéraire* for January–
February 1894, how Vuillard set a green lampshade above a
red tablecloth.

Lugné-Poe had Symbolist principles and liked an un-
cluttered stage He also had Maeterlinck at his shoulder, and
Maeterlinck had very strong ideas about the future of the
theatre. At the present time Maeterlinck's name would
empty any theatre in the English-speaking world, but in
1894 he was listened to with awe. After the publication of
La Princesse Maleine in 1890 there had been many an argument in Paris as to whether Maeterlinck was better than
Shakespeare, beyond question, or simply just as good. All
this would be a matter of the merest historical curiosity if
it were not that Maeterlinck's views as to the quintessence of
the drama were very important to Lugné-Poe and do also,
in point of fact, correspond to the impact of some of the
most beautiful of Vuillard's paintings in the 1890s: *Married
Life*, of 1894, for one, and *The Salon with Three Lamps, rue
Saint-Florentin*, for another.

Maeterlinck wanted to do away with the idea of the
theatre as a place where things happened in an obviously
'dramatic' way. '*The Master Builder*', he wrote in April 1894,
'is one of the first of those modern plays which take ordinary
motionless life for their subject and reveal it to us in all its
gravity, all its clandestine poignancy.' The theatre of action
was based on a primitive and incomplete notion of life; and
the real hero was not Othello or Coriolanus but the man
who sat quietly in an armchair, with the lamplight falling
on the table beside him, while all the laws of life combined
to dictate his destiny. The inner life was the only real life:
all else was posturing.

How far Lugné-Poe managed to bear this out in his productions at the Théâtre de l'Œuvre, we cannot say. But a
painting like *Married Life* has precisely the elements which
Maeterlinck called for: the silence, the half-light, the
tensions buried below the point of visibility. The stage is
set with a richness which the Théâtre de l'Œuvre could not
have afforded and might not even have approved; wall-
paper, tablecloth and patterned dress rhyme most artfully,
and the lights of Paris no less artfully contrast with the stillness of the indoor scene. Vuillard the dramatist has no finer
monument than this painting, which speaks to us like a

In Front of the House   1898

NET PANELS

In the Garden   1898

DESMARAIS PANELS   Stroking the Dog   18

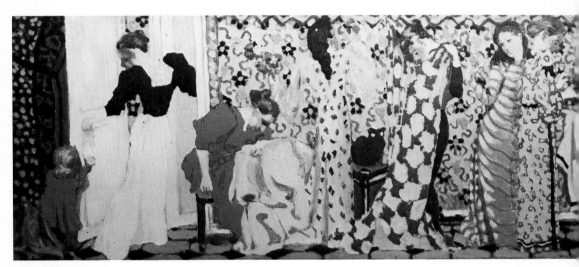

A Dressmaker's Workshop   1892

A Game of Badminton   1

Gardening 1892

Dressmaker's Workshop II 1892

Nursemaids and Children in a Public Garden 1892

THE PUBLIC GARDEN

Out Walking   1894

Asking Questions   1894

The Nursemaids 1894

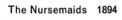

Little Girls Playing 1894

The First Steps 1894

The Conversation (Women on a Bench)   1894

The Red Sunshade   1894

Under the Trees 1894

The Two Schoolboys 1894

Music 1896

Dressmaking 1896

PEOPLE IN ROOMS

Library 1896   The Drawing-room 1896

Scene from *Le Malade Imaginaire* by Molière   1912

Marthe Mellot in her Dressing-room   1912

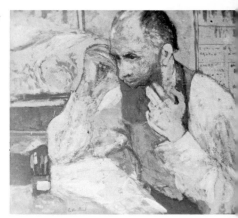

Lugné-Poe in his Dressing-room   1912

The Puppet Show on the Champs-Elysées   1912

Scene from *Le Petit Café* by Tristan Bernard   1912

Bouquets of Flowers and Theatrical Posters   1912

Scene from Massenet's opera *Grisélidis* (?)   1912

Scene from Débussy's opera *Pelléas et Mélisande*   1912

The Salle des Caryatides   1921

The Salle La Caze   1921

The Salle Clarac   1922

Vuillard's Chimneypiece   1922

A Statuette on Vuillard's Chimneypiece   1922

The Department of Sculpture   1922

47

scene from an unwritten play by Chekhov. Equally, the *Salon with Three Lamps* is a small miracle of suggestion: even more than *Married Life* it puts us in mind of evenings in the theatre when great acting makes silence and immobility more eloquent than soliloquy.

The Maeterlinckian moment was no more than a moment in Vuillard's career. He was very good at the hooded lighting which Maeterlinck called for, and he could suggest that a figure sleeping in a comfortable armchair was as much the centre of the world as Victor Hugo's Ruy Blas in full cry. But fundamentally Vuillard's own nature stood in the way of complete identification with Maeterlinck's ideas. The impalpable and the imperceptible were all very well, but the material of everyday life was also there, to be handled as Molière had handled it. It might be true, in one sense, that our destinies were played out in a Nordic twilight, essence against essence, spirit against invisible spirit. But meanwhile there was a good meal on the stove, and amusing things were being said, and people were getting on with life much as they had always done, and on every hand there was something to be looked at, and something to be got down on paper, and much to rejoice at in the play of one individual nature against another. Vuillard was not vivacious in society, but in his work he had the kind of sharp-focused understanding that is more enlivening, in the end, than any amount of boisterous high spirits. The particular won out, in his art, against the general.

We can see from the programmes for the Théâtre de l'Œuvre that he was loyal to Lugné's general policy: play after play is announced by a shadowy group of human beings, barely to be distinguished from their environment and huddled together as if all conversation between them had long come to an end. But Vuillard's own nature was calling the while for what Malvolio calls 'daylight and champaign'; and that was precisely what he went out for when he was invited, in 1893, to paint nine large panels for Alexandre Natanson's house at what is now 60 avenue Foch. They were completed along with so much else, in 1894. It was a misfortune for Vuillard, and for French art, when these decorations, *The Public Garden*, were sold off in 1929. They are reassembled in this book, but in life they can never be got together again. One could curse the turn of fate by which the panel now in Brussels and the panel now in Cleveland, Ohio, are so far apart, since the one can hardly be understood without the other, so close is the correspondence between the settings (taken in both cases from the Tuileries gardens) and so fastidious the interplay between the ragamuffins on the right and the solitary little girl on

Programme: *Beyond Human Strength* (Bjornson) 1894 (cat. 123)

Programme: *Beyond Human Strength*, part 2 (Bjornson) 1897 (cat. 124)

Programme: *Rosmersholm* (Ibsen) 1893 (cat. 125)

Programme: *Pillars of Society* (Ibsen) 1896 (cat. 126)

◀ Place Vintimille 1   1907–08

◀ Place Vintimille 2   1907–08

the left. Jacques Salomon reminds us that at the time of this commission Vuillard and his mother were living only a yard or two from the rue d'Alger, which runs south towards the Tuileries, so that Vuillard had his models directly to hand. We can also agree with M. Salomon that in *The Conversation*, now in Paris, there is a delectable veracity about the three *commères* as they while away the afternoon on their bench. 'Vuillard did not invent', Jacques Salomon says, 'the ungloved left hand of the lady on the right, or her neighbour's vacuous expression. Elsewhere, Vuillard has allowed his imagination free play; the sunlight, for instance, fulfils a decorative purpose as it spreads itself across the foreground. That same sunlight is kept at a distance, however, when it comes to the white umbrella, which merely pretends to shade the sleeping child and in reality is there merely to make the picture more amusing.'

Thadée Natanson had every reason to know about these decorations, and it was his opinion that the nine panels for Alexandre Natanson were presaged in the big painting which now belongs to Mr and Mrs William B. Jaffe, *The Square* (1894). Living as we do in an age when formalist criticism makes all the running and references to subject-matter make an impression, almost, of obscenity, it is not a bad thing to turn back and see what Vuillard's friends and contemporaries made of his paintings. Here, therefore, is the entry for *The Square* from the catalogue of the Thadée Natanson sale, 13 June 1908:

'*The Square*. Beneath trees now tired by the summer, the population of a Parisian square. In the foreground a house-maid in apron and striped uniform, sitting on a bench, watches over a whole pack of children at play, among them a baby squatting on the ground and a little girl in her school overall. In the middleground, some iron chairs; a conversation is in progress between an old lady and a man in a battered straw hat. To the right, people are walking at their ease all the way from the path to the houses which border the square. To the left a parterre of flowers and beyond it a little frieze of people sitting down and beyond that, once again, the houses that overlook the square.

'It should be noted that this painting is the first and no doubt the most audacious of a series of large paintings in the same medium – *peinture à la colle* – all of them painted as mural decorations. In particular, *The Square* served as a starting point for those whose motifs are borrowed from one or another of the gardens of Paris. All the variations which came later are already here in strength, and *The Square* is a dictionary of the ornamental motifs which can be drawn from foliage, from the fabric of a woman's slipper, from the outline of an iron chair, from the scalloped outline of a herbaceous border, etc.

'On an armature of browns, greens of one kind and another stand out, bordered with red; in the centre of the painting a sharp accent of blue stands out above everything else. To right and to left, two yellows lean inwards. The complicated outline of the trees against the sky contrasts with the tonal unity of the foreground.'

Both *The Square* and its successors were far more ambitious than any previous paintings by Vuillard. Not only were they larger and more complex, but they got clear away from the narrow ledge of space with which he had been dealing. They dealt in a deep space, and a space plotted and replotted and related in several cases to a colossal sky. Vuillard could not have done them without careful preparation. He did them in the technique called *peinture à la colle* which he had developed while working in the theatre. (Jacques Salomon gives an exact description of this technique on pages 137–40.) He used the humblest possible colours, bought for next to nothing from the all-purpose chemist's on the corner: 'les verts anglais, le bleu charron et le blanc de Meudon en pain'. As for his subjects, he saw no reason to branch out into mythology, or literature, or the Bible: Paris was quite good enough.

But there remained the question of style. He had not forgotten Maurice Denis's pronouncements of 1890, even if he had never taken to the idea of the 'flat surface' in a doctrinaire way. In the Desmarais decorations he had evaded the issue of depth by choosing subject-matter which did not really exist in depth: where the middle distance appeared at all, it appeared in a theatrical way, as if a painted scene were giving an illusion of distance to a stage that was no more than two paces deep. In the decorations for Alexandre Natanson something different was called for. The linear arabesque of the Desmarais decorations would not serve to hold such large and such thickly detailed paintings together; nor would the melodious clash, common to many of the delectable small paintings of the 1890s, of one petal- or comma-like patch of bright colour against another. Paintings done *à la colle* have quite a different resonance from paintings done in oils: they have, in fact, a subdued inner glow, a matt, felted, contained eloquence which suited Vuillard exactly and is quite different from the dash and dazzle of virtuoso oil-painting. The Desmarais panels owe much of their magic to the natural vivacity of oils: that vivacity could play no part in thè new series.

Jacques Salomon had it from Vuillard himself that he looked closely at Puvis de Chavannes's frescoes, in the

Self-portrait in a mirror, 1914

Vuillard and Roussel with Aristide Maillol

Panthéon, on the life of St Genevieve, and that he had studied reproductions of the fourteenth-century frescoes in the Tour de la Garde-Robe in the Palais des Papes in Avignon. These show a series of pastoral scenes – fishing, fruit-picking, bird-catching, swimming – and they are believed to have been the work of French artists who had seen Arras tapestries and adapted them to painting. Vuillard was very fond of going to see the *Dame à la Licorne* tapestry in the Musée de Cluny, and there is no doubt that in a later series of decorations – those done for Dr Vaquez in 1896 – the memory of *mille-fleur* tapestries played a substantial role. But in 1894 he invoked a great French artist of a much later date, one who was still very much alive, in fact: Claude Monet.

Vuillard's basic problem in *The Public Garden* was to reconcile the nimble-witted graphic style of the human figures with the representation of nature. This had been a hot issue in French painting since the middle of the 1860s, when Monet in preparing his *Déjeuner sur l'herbe* did much of the work out of doors in bright sunlight, with results very different from those achieved by Manet in his famous painting of the same name. Whether or not to start, in such cases, from figures posed indoors was a question on which Courbet, Manet and Monet all had very strong views. The surviving fragments of Monet's *Déjeuner sur l'herbe*, painted at Chailly-en-Bière in 1865–66, and the almost equally large *Women in a Garden*, painted for Bazille at Ville d'Avray in 1867, do undeniably look like the ancestors of certain panels in *The Public Garden*; but Vuillard, for all his temperamental discretion, was very much more imperious in his way of reordering Nature to suit his purpose.

That he should have thought anything at all of the Impressionists was heresy to many of his friends. Direct sensation played no part in their ideas; Vuillard disliked anything that he considered arbitrary or merely willed. Aristide Maillol defined the difference when he wrote to Maurice Denis, some years later: 'I know that Vuillard is not one of us. He does not share the ideas which have come down to us from Gauguin – or, rather, he sees other things. We shall never see alike, and we shall never agree with Vuillard, because he thinks of Gauguin as a pedant.' To the end of his life Maurice Denis believed that painters had a duty to react strongly against Impressionism. In September 1943, more than half a century after his manifesto in *Art et critique*, he had this to say in his diary: 'Went to Emile Bernard's exhibition. No one reacted against Impressionism more strongly than he. No "sensations" in his work, and no "windows open on to nature". Our generation will have been that of the Notion of the picture. Others have pushed that notion as far as abstract art. Bernard made museum art out of it.'

Both Maillol and Denis were, of course, writing at times when Vuillard's work had taken turns unforeseeable in 1894; but it was already clear in 1894 that his was not a doctrinaire nature. He weighed all previous achievements on their merits and without regard for aesthetic loyalty-oaths. If Monet could help him with *The Public Garden*, so much the better. If life as it presented itself before his eyes was richer, more vivid, more fertile in poetic or amusing conjunctions than life as filtered through 'the Notion of the picture', Vuillard was quite happy to drop the Notion overboard.

He did not, in short, confine himself to any one set of ideas. From 1894 onwards he had, also, a greatly extended set of social possibilities, in that he became close to *La Revue Blanche*, with all that that implied in the way of amusing and rewarding frequentations.

La Revue Blanche is much talked about, but almost never read. Copies are very rare, to begin with, and a complete run almost impossible to find. Founded by Alexandre and Thadée Natanson in 1891, it was for eleven years the best periodical of its kind that has ever been published. By this I mean that literature, art and music were represented by people who in many cases were men of individual genius: and that the magazine covered in ideally lively and far-ranging style that complex of activities which, taken together, constitutes the *Zeitgeist*. It was not simply the fact that the Berlin Philharmonic Orchestra's visit to Paris was reported by Debussy, or that the frontispiece was by Vuillard or Bonnard, or that the new poem was Mallarmé's 'Tennyson', or that Tolstoy and Nietzsche were honoured guests from abroad, or that the new young French author was André Gide (with 'Paludes'). It was that the magazine had the mark of the Lycée Condorcet, where the pupils were expected to know about everything without ever appearing to do any work. *La Revue Blanche* carried articles on antisemitism in central Europe, for instance, and on a significant lock-out in a brush factory at Tracy-le-Mont (Oise). It was as interested in Bismarck's birthday as in the new opera by Mascagni, on which F. T. Marinetti, who was to be the founder of Futurism, reported from La Scala. Thadée Natanson's first article on art, in 1893, had to do with Utamaro and Hiroshige; and any reader who took *La Revue Blanche* for a review of an other-worldly aesthetical character would have acknowledged his mistake after working through the very long articles in which the aesthetician Charles Henry discussed the question, 'How should a bicyclist train for maximum endurance?'

Programme for a triple bill (Banz, de Régnier and Strindberg) 1894 (cat. 127)

Vuillard and Roussel with Claude Monet at Giverny, 1923

Thadée Natanson, Félix Vallotton and Romain Coolus, with Cipa Godebski (standing)

Marthe Mellot

A picnic at the Thadée Natansons', c. 1898. Left to right: Vallotton, Vuillard, Stéphane Natanson, Marthe Mellot, Thadée Natanson, Misia Natanson. Standing: Misia's brother Cipa Godebski

Vuillard was introduced to *La Revue Blanche* by Pierre Véber, yet another schoolmate from the Lycée Condorcet. He soon became fast friends with the Natansons, with Misia, the wife of Thadée Natanson, and with the contributors to the magazine and their entourage. With some of those who wrote for *La Revue Blanche* – with Romain Coolus, for instance, and with Tristan Bernard – the friendship lasted a lifetime. With others – Toulouse-Lautrec, for one – there was no great affinity of interests, but Vuillard retained from Lautrec's acquaintance the vivid memories which are reprinted on pages 102–05. Most of the people concerned were in their twenties: the general secretary of the review was Félix Fénéon, the friend and champion of Seurat, and Léon Blum, later to be Prime Minister of France, was a regular contributor. Beyond question the senior held most in honour was Mallarmé, whose death in 1898 was a cruel blow both to the magazine and to the community of private relationships which had formed and re-formed around it.

Vuillard was first mentioned in *La Revue Blanche* in April 1893, when Thadée Natanson reviewed a show at Le Barc de Boutteville's in which Vuillard's *Two Little Girls* was included. 'If M. Vuillard goes on refusing to exhibit,' Natanson wrote, 'we shall suspect him of coquetry – or, rather, we should so suspect him if we did not know that his scruples are quite genuine.' In January 1894 Vuillard designed the frontispiece for the magazine; thereafter he can be considered as an intimate of the Natansons – above all, perhaps, of Misia Natanson, later to become the wife successively of Alfred Edwards the newspaper proprietor and of the painter José María Sert. Her drawing-room in the rue Saint-Florentin, and her country houses at Valvins and later at Villeneuve-sur-Yonne, are familiar to all students of Vuillard's work. Misia was still quite a young girl at the time when Vuillard met her. When she came to write her memoirs, more than fifty years later, she was old, blind and poor, and hardly one of the men who had so much admired her was left alive. In the circumstances it would be unreasonable to expect of her fascinating little book that it should be as reliable as the Channel Pilot. When she speaks of having 'bought a hundred and fifty of van Gogh's paintings, to help his widow' or identifies Guillaume Apollinaire in his beginnings as 'a young man from Prague, a schoolmaster there' we cannot help remembering that van Gogh died a bachelor and that Apollinaire never went to Prague. Misia's own story is so extravagant as almost to defy further exaggeration, right from the moment when her mother died while giving birth to her, in St Petersburg, after having pursued her straying husband through the snows to Tsarskoe Selo. In whatever she did, from infancy onwards, she attracted the attention of whomever was top man in the field in question. Liszt took her on his lap, while sitting at the piano, and made her play a piece which she characteristically identifies as 'Beethoven's Bagatelle in C flat'. '"If only I could still play like that," said the great old man as he helped me back to the floor.' Later, when she was just fifteen, Thadée Natanson asked her to marry him, and she accepted. It was Gabriel Fauré, that time, who burst into tears and begged her to stick to her career as a pianist. '"Don't do this to me," he begged.'

Misia was married three months later, and during the first years of La Revue Blanche life was really very pleasant for this podgy little Slav, with her impulsive and spendthrift ways, her genuine gift for the piano, her starling chatter and her craving for the company of clever and distinguished men. Her house at Valvins was next to Mallarmé's; her apartment in the rue Saint-Florentin – with its salon aux trois lampes, perpetuated in a painting by Vuillard – became familiar to everyone in Paris who was a partisan of the new and the good. In one way and another she became a friend of Mallarmé, Verlaine, Paul Valéry, Bonnard, Jules Renard, Colette and Alfred Jarry. She was the only woman present when Debussy played Pelléas et Mélisande, on an upright piano, singing all the roles himself, to a small group of friends. She and her husband went to Oslo with Lugné-Poe to meet Ibsen. It might have been no more than an overplus of social energy; but in point of fact she was responding in prescient style to the great cry of 'Live all you can!' which was shortly to irradiate The Ambassadors of Henry James.

Among all the men whom she knew, Vuillard had a special place in her affections. 'Our understanding was an unspoken one,' he wrote to her many years later, 'but none the less precious for that.' According to her account, Vuillard was the loyal friend who kept her company in Vienna when her marriage to Thadée was being broken up by a demoniacal millionaire; and, again according to her account, it was Vuillard who, without a word spoken or a gesture made, offered her in a beetroot-field by the Yonne 'the most beautiful declaration of love ever made to me'.

Be that as it may, Vuillard seems to have felt in her presence what he later called 'the security and the assurance of a perfect understanding'. And the paintings which relate to her environment do undeniably have a relaxed, free-flowing quality. They also partake quite distinctly of what could be called the aesthetic of La Revue Blanche. The modernity which the magazine aimed for was above all the modernity

Bonnard and Vuillard with Roussel and his daughter Annette, outside the Panthéon

Annette Salomon, *née* Roussel

Stéphane Mallarmé

of Mallarmé, who was its best-loved contributor and the subtle spirit behind many of its forays into literature, music and art. Vuillard would seem to have known Mallarmé, if not from 1891 onwards, at any rate soon after. It was traditional that very bright young men from the Lycée Condorcet should graduate, as it were, to regular attendance at Mallarmé's Tuesday evenings in the rue de Rome; but it was not until he began to spend much of each summer at Valvins – from 1895 onwards, that is to say – that Vuillard saw Mallarmé regularly. Even then, I suspect that there was no real intimacy between them; Mallarmé is, at any rate, one of the few writers well known to Vuillard of whom no substantial portrait exists. Nor is there an interior of Mallarmé's little house: simply one or two small paintings in which Vuillard restricted himself, with characteristic discretion, to hinting at the look of its exterior.

On the other hand, there is the famous and enigmatic episode of *Hérodiade*. Beyond a doubt, Mallarmé hoped that Vuillard would illustrate the poem in an edition to be published by Vollard. A letter from Mallarmé to Vollard makes this absolutely clear. And *Hérodiade* for Mallarmé, was not a poem among many others. It was the poem which he most wanted to complete; the poem which he had had in hand since 1864; the poem which was to be on his desk on the day he died. Already in 1864, when he was only twenty-two, he saw it as the supreme challenge: 'If I don't bring it off, I'll never touch a pen again.' Writing to Henri Cazalis in October of that year he said: 'I've really got down to work. I've at last begun my *Hérodiade*. It's terrifying, because I'm inventing a language which has to spring from a new notion of poetry. I could define that new notion in two words: *Don't paint the thing itself. Paint the effect it produces.* The lines must be made up not of words, but of intentions, and each phrase must efface itself before the sensations concerned. I *want* – for the first time in my life – I *want to bring it off.*'

This was an ambition which Mallarmé was to pursue till his dying day, and it was one that in certain respects runs parallel to Vuillard's. Mallarmé's use of the word *peindre* – 'Paint the effect it produces' – may or may not have carried with it an allusion to the act of painting with brushes and paint. He was not at that time close to any particular painter – his friendship with Manet began ten years later – and painting itself was of course in a very different condition from that which could be ascribed to it in the mid-1890s. What he wrote to Cazalis can be read as a reference to pure Impressionism; but there is evidence from the 1890s that Mallarmé's ideas had much in common with Vuillard's procedures in the shadowy, self-echoing interiors of the *Revue Blanche* period. In March 1891, he said to an interviewer: 'Once an object is named, three-quarters of the satisfaction which the poem has to offer is lost. The poet should *suggest it*: that is his aim.'

The point, here, is that in his later years Vuillard did a great deal of naming. Late portraits like the *Anna de Noailles* were built up in inventory style. ('For Heaven's sake put away that cold cream!', Madame de Noailles once said to her maid, 'You know how Monsieur Vuillard never leaves anything out.') It was in the 1890s that he gave suggestion freer play: not always, by any means, but in the tranced lamplit interiors which, once again, run parallel to Mallarmé. The Mallarmé in question is the one who wrote in January 1893 that 'Something near to the creative act' – I am here paraphrasing a highly elliptic original – 'is the attempt to evoke an object by placing it deliberately in shadow and referring to it allusively and never by its name.' The evidence for Vuillard's having been directly influenced by Mallarmé is purely inferential; no letters seem to have passed between them, and there is no record of any significant exchange in conversation. Vuillard was present at Valvins when Mallarmé gave a first reading of 'Un coup de dés'; but Jacques Salomon tells us that he was completely bemused by the experience and 'would do no more than smile when we asked what effect the reading had had upon him'.

He was also put off, it would seem, by the awe, genuine but none the less oppressive, with which Mallarmé was treated by visitors to his Tuesday evenings in the rue de Rome. What Vuillard liked was what we see pictured in his work of the 1890s: a quiet evening among equals, in which everyone was free to talk or not, as he pleased, and the lamps were never too bright, and the new books were spread out on the table, and clever men and pretty women were completely at ease with one another. Nobody had to show off, nobody deferred unduly to anyone else, nobody was in a hurry to leave. He found evenings of this sort at the Thadée Natansons' during the years immediately preceding Mallarmé's death; and when those evenings were summer evenings at Valvins Mallarmé was very often there.

Vuillard admired Mallarmé the writer to the extent of copying passages from his work into his notebooks and being able to quote a number of lines by heart; and 'Mallarméan' is one of the adjectives which can usefully distinguish the paintings of the 1890s from those which followed. Mallarmé gave him a first edition of *Divagations*, and Vuillard made some sketches in the margins of it. Mallarmé

A game of chess at Amfreville, in Normandy

In the little sitting-room in the rue de Naples

Mallarmé's house at Valvins

was hopeful in May 1898 that Vuillard would illustrate *Hérodiade*; but within three months Mallarmé was dead, and Vuillard was one of the thirty or so people who followed his coffin to the little churchyard. Claude Roger-Marx has suggested that Vuillard was deterred from attempting to illustrate *Hérodiade* by the failure of Toulouse-Lautrec's *Histoires naturelles*. But it seems to me that the reasons were probably more complex.

Vuillard was conscientiousness personified. He took untold pains over the *Landscapes and Interiors* series, first shown at Vollard's in February 1899, and he was careful in that series to restrict himself to subject-matter of a kind he knew intimately. Unlike Bonnard, he was not an illustrator by nature, and in later years he turned down the idea of illustrating *Un Amour de Swann*, though one can think of few people so well qualified to evoke the Paris which Proust sets before us. The subject-matter of *Hérodiade* was a very long way from his normal preoccupations; and the particular tone of the poem, with its recurrent allusions to snow, ice, glaciers, and landscapes gone dead and cold, and its persistent atmosphere of cold and damp and decay – all this would have been foreign to Vuillard. Even the interior in the opening scene ran contrary to his inclinations, with its accents of snow-white and mother-of-pearl. It is difficult to imagine Vuillard making a go of it; the Mallarmé whose conversation he enjoyed at Valvins was more probably the Mallarmé who had an eye as sharp as Vuillard's own for the peculiarities of human behaviour. That other Mallarmé once said of a group of English tourists that, with their lorgnettes each in a leather sheath, they reminded him of 'the astronomer-herdsmen of Chaldea'.

Vuillard in the 1890s was, as I have tried to indicate, very much in touch with his time. There was nothing provincial or peripheral or belated about his involvement with the new plays, the new books or the new music. He knew the best actors and the best actresses, he heard the best conversation, and he was a freeman of that perennial and in large degree Jewish department of Parisian society in which the doctor, the merchant banker, the editor of the best new magazine, the playwright, the amusing kept woman and the rising politician enjoy one another's company. He knew all this from the inside, with never a hint of the *arriviste* or the bemused young man from out of town. When van Gogh, for instance, painted a plaster statuette and a couple of new French novels in 1887 he was concerned to identify the books in question as two of the successes of the day: Maupassant's *Bel-Ami* and the Goncourt brothers' *Germanie Lacerteux*; the cast, also, took on at his hands a poignancy in which were mingled the dream of classic art, the bodily charms of the living Parisiennes whom van Gogh never got to make love with, and the struggles to find a style, appropriate to the current state of art, for one of art's permanent subjects. The very awkwardness of the picture bespoke the moral struggle within it.

Vuillard did, in point of fact, encounter private difficulties of an extreme sort while working up to achievements which look to us quite spontaneous. But when he included a cast from the antique in his paintings (as he did, for instance, in *Madame Val* in 1920) he did it with complete assurance, and with a sidelong irony; in the example I have just mentioned there is the gentlest possible oblique mischief in the contrast between Madame Val's portly outline and the hallowed stance of the Venus de Milo. And when he painted a pile of new books in the *Interior with Six Characters* which is now in the Kunsthaus in Zürich it never occurred to him to spell out their titles. They emerge, rather, as a chromatic explosion: a still-life the more eloquent for being expressed in Mallarmé's terms, with everything suggested and nothing directly named. We may remember in this context what Aldous Huxley had to say in *The Doors of Perception* about the way books looked to him after he had taken mescalin: 'they glowed, when I looked at them, with brighter colours, a profounder significance. Red books, like rubies; emerald books; books bound in white jade; books of agate, of aquamarine, of yellow topaz; lapis lazuli books whose colour was so intense, so intrinsically meaningful, that they seemed to be on the point of leaving the shelves to thrust themselves more insistently on my attention.'

Aldous Huxley was a very great admirer of Vuillard, but he saw him in terms of mystical experience: 'the Dharma-Body manifested in a bourgeois bedroom, the Absolute blazing away in the midst of some stockbroker's family in a suburban garden'. This was certainly no part of Vuillard's intention, and it would doubtless have amazed him quite as much as the famous first reading of 'Un coup de dés'. Vuillard's subject was, on the contrary, the here-and-now. If many of the paintings of the 1890s have unearthly overtones for us, it is because Vuillard's sense of tone at that time was uniquely persuasive. A sense of celestial security comes over us as he re-creates the world, touch by touch, in such a way that everything in it harmonizes with every other thing. What in other hands would be a jangle of discordant patterns comes out as a paradise on earth: the world is at one with itself. There is also, in the pictures of that date, the fact that Vuillard discards the classic single-point-of-view perspective. Space does not retreat before us; we can caress it.

Vuillard in his workroom at 26 rue de Calais

Sketch for 'Madame Val Synave'

Roussel and Vuillard at L'Etang-la-Ville, c. 1923

Vuillard remembers the injunction of Maurice Denis; we are as aware of the flat surface as we are of the counter-indications of depth.

Vuillard's vocation during the 1890s was in full evolution. At the dealers', and in the auction-room, we mostly now see what are, at their best, small masterpieces of the apparently informal and the seemingly offhand: tiny panels in which the action scutters off-centre and the image has, even after three-quarters of a century, a startling asymmetry. But Vuillard did not see himself as a miniaturist, and it is an accident of art history that his major works are very much more difficult to see. He could, however, reveal monumental ambitions even when working to the scale of the Japanese prints which he had seen with great profit at the Galerie Bing. An example of this, and a painting which despite its small size is a key work in the development of French painting, is the Colins' *Family at Luncheon* of 1896.

This little picture was painted eleven years after van Gogh's *The Potato-Eaters*, nine years after Signac's *Breakfast*, and shortly before Matisse's *The Dessert*. It shares with all three of the others a wish to give monumentality to every-day life; and, as against Vuillard's earlier domesticities, it reveals a much greater concern with three-dimensional representation. The woman at the table on the right is as sculptural as her counterpart in *The Potato-Eaters*; the carafes have the sacramental quality of the household objects in Signac's big picture; and the picture as a whole foreshadows the pyramidal composition of the Matisse, just as the cluster of carafes, plates, knives and forks and glasses on the table creates a deep space of the kind which Matisse was to exploit in *The Dessert*.

But the crucial fact for Vuillard's evolution is that he allied himself to recent tradition without giving up the marks of his own style as it had previously existed. He set up a vertical/horizontal grid against which his figures were pinned like butterflies on a notice-board. He drew the central figure in profile with a jagged, fast-moving line that is an after-echo of Art Nouveau. If the right-hand seated woman is like an up-graded potato-eater, the left-hand one has the witty, discreetly caricatural look of Vuillard's widows of a year or two before. The figure in the background is the figure that comes round the screen in Vuillard's dressmaking subjects; and the alternations of light and dark, void and solid, rectilinear and all-over-patterned, are precisely as they had been in the big decorations. In the *Family at Luncheon* Vuillard offers himself as a candidate for membership of the French school; this is interior-painting as it had been understood since the days of Louis le Nain, with a classical equilibration of mathematical design and humane observation.

A candidature of this kind was not in fashion among Vuillard's friends in the second half of the 1890s. Vuillard was, in any case, something of a mystery to them. As he may also, at times, be something of a mystery to ourselves, and as we have to wait until 1990 for the unsealing of his diaries, a great importance attaches to a letter dated 1897 in which he unburdened himself to Maurice Denis.

In September 1897 Maurice Denis had just come back to Paris after spending the summer in Brittany. Clearly it was worrying him that Vuillard was tending more and more towards what was often called the 'cut from nature' – i.e. the fragment of life observed *sur le vif* and set down in the directest possible terms. This was contrary to Denis's beliefs as they had been set out in the manifesto of 1890; judged by those standards it was, in his view, a regressive attitude. The picture should be, but in Vuillard's case was not, an autonomous object in which the artist had his way with Nature.

'Such is the multitude of motifs which Nature sets before us', Denis wrote in his diary, 'that if we begin to identify with the sights of everyday we shall never attain to a reasoned professionalism. We shall never have time, for one thing. Eventually, and with practice, the habit of identifying with what we see makes everything expressive – i.e. suitable subject-matter for painting. When I am tired at the end of the day and go out to take the air I see more subjects in the course of a single walk than Claude Lorrain or Poussin could paint in a whole year. In the same way Vuillard, in his determination to take note of everything, finishes nothing.

'It is not that we should try to work faster while painting, but rather that we should think more slowly. I told Vuillard that we don't stick to any one thing long enough. We complain when we come back from a month in the country with nothing done. Yet with a genuinely fecund artist – Rubens, say – a change of location has no effect whatever on his output. I also spoke to Vuillard about the notion of Fame. None of us believes in *la Gloire* any longer, but it must have been of some use to the unhurrying painters of days gone by. In brief, this craving to note down the sights of everyday is simply the result of outdated ideas about fidelity to Nature. That one primordial blunder is at the root of all our difficulties. An ambition other than "self-expression" is needed before a man can create something really substantial.'

Seventy years of hindsight allow us to suggest that Vuillard had, on the contrary, already created something

Preliminary drawing for 'Annette Dreaming', *c.* 1918

Annette Roussel, *c.* 1906

61

'really substantial' by the autumn of 1897. But what Denis had in mind was, no doubt, that Vuillard's methods were primarily perceptual. He had a darting, elliptic, first-hand way with experience and was not at all doctrinaire. Denis by 1897 had proved that he could order experience in a large-scale, systematic way – above all in the seven very large panels, *St Hubert's Hunt*, for Denys Cochin – and one can understand that Vuillard's informal procedures seemed to him altogether too obsequious to the passing moment. The conceptual element needed stiffening, in Denis's view; and when he was staying in Rome in February of the following year he unburdened himself in a letter to Vuillard.

Denis found Rome a most challenging experience. Not only was there almost too much to see and to master, but Rome had a particular lesson: 'In Rome', he noted on 26 January 1898, 'it no longer occurs to me to make little notes in my sketchbook. Rome puts me in mind of great undertakings, pictures thought through and thought out from end to end. Raphael and Titian for the figure, Claude Lorrain for landscape. The kind of thing that calls for an interminable patience and has nothing contingent about it.' André Gide was with him, and they had day-long conversations about how best to go forward from Impressionism. Denis's diary gives the gist of their talk: 'The example of the masters: concentration upon major works only; no dissipating of effort on a multitude of subsidiary projects.' 'Charm is not enough.' 'We must have the courage to resist two things: (1) our over-excited sensibilities; (2) our public, and our dealers, who ask us for five-minute "impressions" of art. Life might seem longer – who knows? – where now it seems to us desperately short. Life would grow in size, just as our works would grow in size.'

There was no chance of persuading Vuillard to Rome – he was, all his life, too much the complete Frenchman to have time for Abroad – but at least he could be got at by letter. It was Raphael, more than anyone, who prompted the outburst.

'That man is unbelievable,' Denis wrote to Vuillard on 15 February 1898. 'In twenty years he did everything that could be done with art. He tried everything. He succeeded with everything. His versatility is beyond belief.

'And it's there that I've had a running mental quarrel with you, these last few days. I think we make a great mistake in demanding of a work of art that it should seduce us from the outset and give us pleasure of an immediate sort. How many mediocre, ephemeral, pointless paintings do just that? How many profoundly moving paintings do nothing of the sort? We are much at fault in all this. Fashion leads us astray; and, with fashion, an exaggerated reaction against decadent academic art. It's time we woke up to it. Nothing could be more ugly than the *Last Judgment* in the Sistine Chapel, and yet it is one of the great paintings of all time. It's the same thing with the Raphaels in the Vatican. At a first visit, one would exchange the whole lot for just one gold-ground painting that is unambiguous, expressive and at one with itself; yet when one comes to love them one ranks them above everything else. You will agree that one could say the same of Poussin and Ingres, who are no more than Raphael's descendants.

'The importance of any given work of art resides in the plenitude of the artist's will and the extent to which he has given all of himself. You soon see in Rome that the painters of the great period, like their admirable followers Poussin and Ingres, thought only of how to have great ideas and carry them through to the end. No place known to me is more directly the antipodes of Impressionism. Delicious as are one's fleeting impressions in Rome, one hardly ever thinks to note them down. What Rome gives us is the strength to embark on paintings like Ingres's *The Vow of Louis XIII*, which take two years to complete. I shall come back to Paris even more convinced of the ideas which I expounded to you while I was preparing my portrait for the last Salon.'

The portrait in question was, conceivably, the considered, measured, majestic double portrait of Maurice Denis and his wife on the terrace of the Villa Montrouge at Fourqueux, which Denis showed at the Société Nationale des Beaux-Arts in 1897. Its steady and unswerving ambitions were certainly distinct from Vuillard's. Denis's letter drew, in any case, a reply by return of post.

'My dear Denis. – The questions which you bring up in your letter are a matter of torture to me in my life, in my work, *everywhere*. I cannot but reply to you at once. Help me please, to make myself clear.

'It is not "while working", as you say, that I think even for a moment of the look of the painting or of its possible immediate charm. Let me generalize and say that I never, in any context, think of my actions in terms of quality. Remember what I'm like, and how shy I am. If I am lucky enough to get down to work at all, it's because I have an idea that I believe in. The quality of the result is neither here nor there, at such times. I take it for granted that it has merit of some kind: a merit that corresponds to the universality or the general importance, of the idea in question. The last thing I think of at such moments is how to seduce the observer or give him immediate pleasure of any kind. I well

Mme Vuillard at breakfast

Mme Vuillard sewing

understand how repulsive such ideas must be to any serious person. When I am at work – how glad you will be to hear this! – I just wouldn't know what you were talking about.

'But when I don't have faith in what I'm doing – well, I go on working, of course. But by fits and starts. You can't imagine how dismally the time passes. My guiding ideas are no more than lightning flashes, even though I don't deny the possibility of a steadier illumination. Forgive this self-analysis – after all, you asked for it. I'll try to get back to where we started from.

'As for that plenitude of the will, that fullness of effort which you speak of, I can imagine what it's like. But, whether from a curable infirmity or an innate weakness of character, I don't often experience it. Yet our two points of view may not be irreconcilable, if you will bear with me. The word "will" has always had a clear and distinct meaning for you. Everything has tended towards it – your nature, your education, your circumstances. Faced with end-products that please you – in my own case, for instance – you attribute them to logical causes of your own devising. But what if you are mistaken? In my case, for instance, there was a moment when everything turned to ashes. It may have been from some inner weakness in myself, or it may have been that principles which had been instilled in me were insufficiently solid. Either way, one thing after another was eliminated, until the group of formulated ideas in which I still believed was reduced to its basic elements. (If I say "formulated", it is because I have, after all, had some experience of life.) A sort of intimate whirlwind took over. The only guide left to me was instinct, pleasure, satisfaction (wherever I could find it). It was at that time that I became over-fond of using words like "delicious" and "delectable". They get the better of me when I get becalmed and can't think how to start working again. The area in which I was quite certain of anything got smaller and smaller; all I could do was the simplest possible kind of work. Luckily I had good friends. They helped me to believe that simple accords of colour or form could be meaningful in themselves. But that – the point at which all I had to do was to write – was only the beginning of a dangerous convalescence.

'Well, enough of that. The important thing is that I had a basis on which to go on painting pictures. And I agreed that that could be called "work". It was work that brought results. It allowed me to put one or two ideas together, in ways that did not too much violate my conviction that everything must be summoned forth from one's own inmost being. (Call it a craving for "originality", "personality" – vanities of one kind and another.) I got from all this the same satisfaction that I got from my first attempts at art. Of course I agree with you that that kind of satisfaction, that specific contentment, can be found in many a different case and can affect many another (and far more complex) character. But, whatever it is, I still need it. So I don't claim to pass any judgments. If I were sensible I'd keep away from people. In that way I should never mislead anyone. Some works of art leave me indifferent; but in my more lucid moments I willingly admit that that indifference is all my own fault. I admit it as a criticism not of the work of art but of my own state of mind.

'To sum up, I have a horror (or, rather, an absolute terror) of general ideas that I have not arrived at by myself. It's not that I deny their validity. I'd rather own up to my shortcomings than pretend to an understanding that I don't really possess. If something comes up that I can enjoy I don't hesitate to enjoy it, believe me. But I am not nearly as mono-lithic as you seem to suppose, and it really surprises me that you should set me up as a mental sparring-partner. A picture that would take two years to paint! I know very well that it would be a great thing to do. I know that there were such things in the past, and that they gave pleasure of a quite exceptional sort – and a sort almost unknown in our own day. My own private obstinacy is that I believe that we know all about that particular pleasure, and that when my moments of weakness and incapacity add up to a certain overplus of depression I shall find myself metamorphosed in such a way that I can discard all outmoded formulae and revert spontaneously to quite another method of work.'

Vuillard ended his letter, as Denis had ended his, with small-talk about the Dreyfus affair. The art world, like every other world, was in a fever of anxiety and self-doubt on that subject. 'In every household,' Vuillard wrote, 'there are violent scenes from time to time. People get quite out of control.' Vuillard had seen the painter Eugène Carrière dining with Georges Clemenceau and the critic Gustave Geffroy; lucky the moment in history when great men of affairs were interested to dine with painters and critics!

Maurice Denis thought it a pity that *La Revue Blanche* and its supporters should have intervened so directly on the side of Dreyfus; and as for Vuillard's ideas about painting, as expressed in the letter I have just quoted, Denis felt that they would lead him straight back to Impressionism. Vuillard would never be progressive for progressiveness's sake, and he would go on worrying away at his gifts until they found whatever kind of expression seemed right to him, irrespective of whether it tallied with what seemed right to his friends.

Paul Cézanne, 1914 (cat. 128)

The Artist's Mother, *c.* 1895 (cat. 129)

Mme Vuillard

Nor was Denis the only friend of Vuillard who doubted, in the late 1890s, that Vuillard was shaping as well as he could have. Signac's diary-entry, reprinted on p. 95, is a vivid reminder of this. To many people he still seemed a miniaturist, a master of the finished picture which, as Signac said, was left in the condition of a sketch. This was especially out of favour with those who believed that the easel-painting was a minor form of art and that the real thing was the mural. Prefacing the catalogue of the Thadée Natanson sale in 1908, the novelist Octave Mirbeau gave late but firm expression to this when he said that 'Vuillard is never more at ease, nor does he ever give us greater pleasure, than when his imagination – "musical" is the word I would choose for it – has ample surfaces at its disposal. Walls are what his magic needs: *il faut des murs à sa magie.*'

Well, he got them. The example set by Alexandre Natanson in 1894, when he commissioned the *Public Garden* series, was followed by others: initially by Dr Vaquez in 1896, and later by the novelist Claude Anet, and by the dramatist Henry Bernstein. There were others: for the bar of the Comédie des Champs-Elysées, for a country house owned by the Bernheims, Paris art dealers, at Villers-sur-Mer, for a country house near Basle in Switzerland, for the new theatre in the Palais de Chaillot in 1937, and finally for the League of Nations building in Geneva (1936–39). Throughout his career, therefore, Vuillard accepted the challenge of the major commission. Some were more successful than others; but the fundamental thing is that Vuillard remained loyal to the idea current in his twenties – and current, also, in the lifetime of his great favourite Le Sueur – that the large decoration was a higher form of art than the easel-painting.

As he got older he manifested another unfashionable belief: that it was the artist's duty to bear witness, in large-scale formal style, and not simply to ravish the senses. In fulfilling this duty he painted pictures which it would never have occurred to Bonnard, for one, to paint: elaborate representations of the Paris Métro, scenes in munition factories during World War I, an *Interrogation of Prisoners*, again between 1914 and 1918, an evocation of a large tea-room, *Le Grand Teddy*, and a number of latter-day *portraits d'apparat*, over which he toiled in traditional style. His masterpiece in the genre is to my mind *Dr Vaquez at the Hôpital Saint-Antoine* of 1921, now in the Académie Nationale de Médecine in the rue Bonaparte. What Vuillard produced is nothing less than a secular Deposition: a majestic formal statement in which his human understanding and his professional skill rival those of Dr Vaquez himself. As in the

1914 portrait *Dr Viau Operating*, Vuillard here kept strictly to fact, and to fact of a particularly cheerless sort: the *mundus muliebris* was many a mile away, and the climate was that of the great medical paintings of the past – notably, perhaps, Thomas Eakins's *The Gross Clinic* of 1875. The scene is timeless, the preoccupations eternal, the un-mannered exposition entirely apt.

In 1896, on the other hand, the Vaquez decorations (not seen in public, by the way, till 1905) were as true to their time as Whistler's *Peacock Room* was true to the mid-1870s. They were the apotheosis of the flat, flower-patterned background; of the imperious play of arabesque against recurrent horizontal; of the deftly placed period detail, the single slender vase in *The Salon*, for instance, with its no less slender flowers; and of the tranced inward stillness, the sense of life being carried forward in silence, which survive as a last legacy of Maeterlinck's fragmented, half-spoken dialogues. Flatness had its last great fling in the Vaquez panels. Based in part, as André Chastel has pointed out, on French tapestries of the fifteenth and sixteenth centuries, and in particular on the *mille-fleur* backgrounds then in favour, they have a quality which is as much sewn as painted: every stitch is equal with every other stitch. Vuillard presents us with an enclosed world in which daylight has no place; he often delighted in juggling with three or four evident sources of light, but in the Vaquez panels there is no such source. A hooded, even, impartial light reinforces the unity of the four scenes; it is not surprising that when they were shown at the Salon d'Automne in 1905, when the revelation of Fauve painting was the sensation of the day, they seemed to stand (as we can see from André Gide's opinion, reprinted on p. 96) for a well-bred, soft-spoken dreamland: an Act V of *Pelléas* in which all would end happily and no one would have to die.

By 1905, however, the world had moved on, and Vuillard had moved with it. There had been important changes in his external life. The milieu of *La Revue Blanche* had come to an end, like the magazine itself; Mallarmé was dead, Toulouse-Lautrec was dead, Misia Natanson was getting divorced from her husband, the salon in the rue Saint-Florentin was disbanded, the unhurried summers at Valvins and Villeneuve-sur-Yonne were a thing of the past. Vuillard had gained, on the other hand, a country base at l'Etang-la-Ville, where K.-X. Roussel, married since 1893 to Vuillard's sister Marie, had taken a house. Bonnard and Vuillard were regular visitors there, and from 1899 until 1914 the three of them showed together at Bernheim-Jeune's. The Bernheims had on their staff at that time a young man called Jos Hessel;

Vuillard, by Roussel, *c.* 1934

Mme Hessel at home, c. 1905

and it happened that in 1900, when Vuillard was visiting Félix Vallotton at Romanel, near Lausanne, he made the acquaintance of Madame Hessel, who for the next forty years was to be one of his closest friends.

Madame Hessel was a tall dark woman of commanding aspect. She was also an admirable *maîtresse de maison*, with all that that implies in the way of resource, love of comfort, and vigilant affection. She was not at all someone to be trifled with. Her husband was already in a good way of business (this we may judge from the look of their apartment on the rue de Rivoli, which Vuillard often painted during the first years of their acquaintance) and his affairs continued to prosper. When he felt like buying a country house, during the war of 1914–18, he sold a Cézanne to pay for it. There was nothing equivocal or underhand about Vuillard's relations with Hessel, and he waxed very angry indeed if anyone chanced to speak disrespectfully of Hessel in his hearing. He travelled in Spain and Holland with the Hessels, he spent a substantial part of each summer with them, and at the end of the day in Paris he could be found in Madame Hessel's salon as often as not. She was a very good friend indeed to Vuillard, and he, in turn, portrayed her at every stage in her life until the summer day, in 1940, when he died while trying to make his way to her house by the sea.

Vuillard's was an independent nature; but people do, even so, take on the colour of those whom they see continually, and there is an evident contrast between Misia Natanson, with her improvident ways, her unfeigned love of music and poetry, her sexy little muzzle and her kaleidoscopic private life, and the majestic figure of Madame Hessel. The Hessel milieu was one in which painters and writers and actors and actresses were welcome, but it was not a milieu to which they were indispensable; nor was it a milieu in which the ideas most naturally in favour were those of the avant-garde. The conversation was very good, but it was not the kind of thing that Vuillard had heard at 28 rue Pigalle, or at the Natansons' in the heyday of *La Revue Blanche*. He had his point of entry, for conversation of that sort, at the Arthur Fontaines', 2 avenue de Villars, where the composer Chausson was a member of the family and Debussy, Gide, Claudel and Francis Jammes were regular callers. What he got from the Hessels was friendship of another kind: indestructible, appreciative, well upholstered, full of a nourished good sense.

Vuillard had never invented a subject in his life; and as he got older the Hessels and their friends assumed an even greater ascendancy in his subject-matter, until, towards the end, when he made his large decoration for the Palais de

Chaillot in 1937, he turned the park of the Hessels' château, Les Clayes, into a background for characters summoned up from the memory of *A Midsummer Night's Dream*. In an unsystematic way he assembled as complete a record as any we have of the way well-to-do people looked and behaved in the France of the Third Republic; already in 1904 Marcel Proust spoke of 'his admirable talent, which has so often kindled my memory'.

At the time of his first meeting with Madame Hessel, Vuillard's vocation was complete. There would always be surprises in his work: pictures where the man of deep concealed feeling took over from the hyper-conscientious craftsman. His mother, until her death in 1928, would provide him with motifs no two of which were ever quite alike. But there was never again a time when, as in the 1890s, nobody could be quite sure which way Vuillard would go next. This was not the kind of career he had in mind. He had settled for the long haul of fact, and he stayed with it to the end. His way of painting *à la colle* allowed of an immensely painstaking technical approach and a super-abundance of reworking. If Signac was able as late as 1898 to scold Vuillard for his lack of attention to detail, he would surely have revised his opinion in the face of the great series of decorations which are remarkable above all for the ease, the freshness and the insatiable appetite with which Vuillard applied himself to the minutiae of fact.

When invited, for instance, to decorate the newly built Comédie des Champs-Elysées in 1913, he could have got away with general indications of the kind that had ornamented his programmes for the Théâtre de l'Œuvre. But twenty years had given him a new set of preoccupations. Two small panels represent his old friend Lugné-Poe and another theatrical friend of hardly shorter standing, Marthe Mellot. The puppet theatre from the Champs-Elysées forms the subject of a tall panel on its own, and marvellous it is to see how Vuillard gives it just that sharpness of colour which is needed to catch our attention. For the four large panels he turned to the theatre as it was at that moment, and to known productions and known performers. The apparatus of illusion – footlights, elaborate scenery, real furniture – allowed him, in the two horizontal panels, just the frieze-like composition, the irrational lighting, and the profusion of droll and often unintended detail which his genius throve upon. One of the plays was Molière's *Le Malade imaginaire*, the other a recent success by Tristan Bernard, another habitué of the Hessels'. Vuillard brought the audience into the picture, too, so that from certain points of view we can mingle the real stall-holders with the painted ones, and the

Mme Hessel at the time of Vuillard's first meeting with her

Mme Hessel, *c.* 1900

Vuillard drawing at his window overlooking the Place Vintimille

Vuillard and his mother at 6 Place Vintimille, 1927

real proscenium arch with the pictured one, and the memory of the voices but lately stilled on the stage with the illusion of the ones that Vuillard all but makes audible to us, so vividly does he catch the look of the actors, and the stance, and their way of catching the *réplique* in mid-air.

Above the bar, Vuillard set two vertical panels of subjects from the repertory of the Opéra-Comique. One we can all recognize: it comes from Debussy's *Pelléas et Mélisande*. The other Jacques Salomon identifies as a scene from Massenet's *Grisélidis*, an opera which of late has found few to champion it. Anyone who doubts that Vuillard was one of the great decorators should go to the dress-circle balcony which looks down on to the bar and note how the panels look as well from above as from below.

People often discuss Vuillard in terms which imply the prefix 'If only . . .': if only he had gone on to invent abstract painting, if only he had continued the Mallarméan vision of the 1890s, if only he had dictated to Nature. And of course art history would have taken a different course if Vuillard had invented abstract painting ten years before Kandinsky. It would also have been different, though less markedly so, if Vuillard had not reverted to the formal devices of an earlier generation after 1900, toiling to give an account, as veracious as he could make it, of complex and often unrewarding visual situations. Truth of humane observation, truth of feeling, the loyal fulfilment of tasks which none but he could have undertaken – all these are qualities now much discounted. People who have learned to read the delicious, elliptic and pictorially irreverent little paintings of the *Revue Blanche* period have a sense of almost bodily oppression when they study the ceremonious late portraits in which space is rendered in conservative style and the errors of tact and taste which abounded in Third Republic interiors are reported faithfully and without comment. Vuillard brought a Tolstoyan fullness and roundness to his account of life in the Place Vintimille; but he also brought a vivacity, an epigrammatic speed and lightness of expression which were specifically his own. He bore witness to Misia as a middle-aged woman, in *The Black Cups*, in an up-to-the-minute interior of the 1920s; to new faces in the theatre – Sacha Guitry, Yvonne Printemps, Jane Renouardt, Elvire Popesco; to younger writers like Jean Giraudoux and older ones hitherto unknown to him, like Paul Léautaud, who in times of stress had kept himself going by selling off odd copies of Vuillard's programmes for the Théâtre de l'Œuvre; to friends grown old – Bonnard, Denis, Roussel, Maillol; and from time to time to the look of himself, for Vuillard was one of the most searching of self-portraitists.

Our generation is not sympathetic to the master-qualities of late Vuillard – the ox-like patience, the steadiness of mind, the determination to take pictorial problems one by one and worry them through to the end. We are more responsive to the 'intimate whirlwind' of which he once wrote to Maurice Denis; and there is no doubt that much of the best art of this century corresponds to what Maurice Denis called for in the 'Definition' of 1890 – 'the universal triumph of the aesthetic imagination over the stupidities of effortful imitation, and the triumph of a feeling for beauty over the false witness of naturalism'. Of course it was easy to call for that at the age of nineteen, and difficult to live up to it for the next fifty years. Certainly Maurice Denis did not carry out his own programme. As for Vuillard, perhaps he turned those bold phrases over and over and decided that the anti-thesis was a false one. Perhaps he thought that 'effortful imitation' need not exclude the triumph of the aesthetic imagination, and that naturalism need not always bear false witness? Perhaps the influence of the Marist Fathers came on strong, in the end, and he found within himself that 'plenitude of the will' which was beyond his reach in the 1890s? Conceivably his diaries will tell us, but I doubt it. Vuillard was the ideal confidant, for other people, but he didn't do much confiding himself. Even his work was kept secret: between 1912 and 1938 he did not once have a one-man show in Paris. There is much to wonder about, as there is also much to wonder at, in the vocation of Edouard Vuillard.

Mme Vuillard at luncheon with her son, 1927

At luncheon

71

Maurice Denis

The Influence of Paul Gauguin

Gauguin died on 8 May 1903. The review L'Occident *had published in March, April and May 1903 a study of his paintings by Armand Seguin. The role of Maurice Denis, writing in the October issue, was, therefore, rather to throw light on the background of Gauguin's career than to attempt a further examination of his work. At a distance of just fifteen years he was able to give what is still the most vivid and authentic account of what happened when Sérusier returned from Brittany with the 'Talisman'.*

Among the young artists who, about 1888, were studying at the Académie Julian, even the most daring were in almost total ignorance of the great movement which, under the name of Impressionism, had recently revolutionized the art of painting. They had not progressed beyond Roll and Dagnan: they admired Bastien-Lepage; they spoke of Puvis with respectful indifference, honestly suspecting that he did not know how to draw. Thanks to Paul Sérusier, who was then student-in-charge of the studio – an office which he filled with dashing eccentricity – our culture was wider than in most official art schools: we talked familiarly of Péladan and Wagner, of the Lamoureux concerts and of decadent literature, with which in fact we were ill acquainted; a pupil of Ledrain's initiated us into Semitic literature, and Sérusier expounded the doctrines of Plotinus and the Alexandrian school to the young Maurice Denis, who was studying philosophy for the *baccalauréat ès lettres*.

It was at the beginning of the autumn term in 1888 that Gauguin's name was first revealed to us by Sérusier, who had just returned from Pont-Aven. He showed us – not without making a certain mystery of it – a cigar-box lid on which we could make out a landscape that was all out of shape and had been built up in the Synthetist manner with patches of violet, vermilion, Veronese green and other colours, all put on straight from the tube and with almost no admixture of white. 'How does that tree look to you?' Gauguin had asked him, looking at a corner of the Bois d'Amour. 'It's a vivid green, isn't it? So take some green, the best green you've got on your palette. And that shadow's blue, really, isn't it? So don't be afraid – make it as blue as you can.'

In this paradoxical and unforgettable form we were presented for the first time with the fertile concept of 'a plane surface covered with colours assembled in a certain order'. Thus we learned that every work of art was a transposition, a caricature, the passionate equivalent of a sensation experienced. This was the beginning of a movement in which H. G. Ibels, Pierre Bonnard, Paul Ranson and Maurice Denis promptly participated.

We began to frequent places quite unknown to our principal, Jules Lefebvre: the *entresol* of Goupil's house on the boulevard Montmartre, where van Gogh's brother showed us not only Gauguins from Martinique but also paintings by

Vincent himself, Monet and Degas; and Père Tanguy's shop in the rue Clauzel, where we discovered Cézanne, to our immense excitement. Sérusier's keen philosophical mind soon transformed Gauguin's slightest words into a scientific doctrine, which made a decisive impression on us. For Gauguin himself was no pedagogue, although he was sometimes thought to be; Lautrec took a malicious pleasure in calling him 'Professor'. On the contrary, he was essentially intuitive. In his conversation as well as in his writings there were felicitous aphorisms, profound perceptions, assertions whose logic astonished us. He only realized this later, I imagine, when having left Brittany, where his disciples foregathered,[1] at the time when literary Symbolism had become a matter of public interest, he recognized his own ideas expressed, in Paris, under the systematic and over-subtle form given them, for instance, by Albert Aurier.

It may not have been Gauguin who invented Synthetism, which through contact with writers developed into Symbolism; on this controversial question Emile Bernard is very positive. But Gauguin was none the less the master, the unquestioned master, whose paradoxes were noted and repeated and who won our admiration by his talent, his fluency, his gestures, his physical strength, his harshness, his inexhaustible imagination, his very strong head for drink and his romantic bearing. The secret of his sway lay in his providing us with one or two very simple, incontestably true ideas at a time when we were totally without guidance. Thus, without ever having sought for beauty in the classic sense of the word, he almost immediately induced us to become concerned with it. He wanted above all to convey character, to express the 'inner idea' even in what was ugly. He was still an Impressionist, but he sought to read the book 'in which the eternal laws of Beauty are written'.[2] He was fiercely individualistic, and yet he clung to popular traditions of the most anonymous, collective sort. We deduced laws, lessons, a method, from these contradictions.

But the Impressionist ideal was by no means obsolete, in those already far-off days. We could still subsist on what we had learnt from Renoir or Degas. Gauguin transmitted their lesson to us, enriched with what he had himself borrowed from the classical tradition and from Cézanne. He revealed Cézanne's achievement to us, not as that of an independent genius, an irregular follower of Manet, but as what it really is: the end-product of long exertion, the necessary result of a great crisis.

Impressionism, as explained by his work and his paradoxes, still meant sunshine, diffused light, freedom of composition, the sense of values as revealed by Corot, a shimmering technique, the love of bright colour, and the influence of Japanese art, which was gradually spreading like a leaven through the whole movement; it was all this, true, but it was something more. Gauguin offered us a twofold heritage.

He freed us from all the shackles that the idea of copying imposed on painters' instincts. In the studios where the crudest realism had replaced the drab academicism of the last pupils of Ingres; where one of our teachers, Doucet, exhorted us to 'heighten the interest' of a subject from Christ's Passion, which had been set us for a sketch, by using photographs of Jerusalem – we aspired to the joy of self-expression which the young writers of the time were so urgently demanding. The theory of equivalents provided us with the means; we had derived it from Gauguin's expressive imagery; he gave us the right to lyricism; and for instance, if it was permissible, when we saw a tree as tawny-red, to paint it vermilion, why should we not exaggerate, in our visual representation of them, those impressions that justify the metaphors of poetry – emphasizing the curve of a beautiful shoulder by distorting it, exaggerating the pearly whiteness of flesh or the stiffness of a branch shaken by no wind?

This explained the whole of the Louvre for us, the Primitives and Rubens and Veronese. Only, we went beyond Gauguin's rudimentary teaching, replacing his over-simple concept of pure colours by that of beautiful harmonies as infinitely varied as nature; we adapted all the resources of our palettes to our various states of mind and feeling; and the things seen which provided our themes were also symbols of our subjective experience. We sought 'equivalents', but in the realm of beauty! . . . Beside us, certain over-conscientious Americans displayed their stupid skill in copying some insignificant model in a drab light. Our eyes were full of the marvels that Gauguin had brought back from Martinique and Pont-Aven: splendid visions, compared with the miserable realities of our official teachers! It was a salutary intoxication, an unforgettable enthusiasm! Moreover Sérusier proved to us by means of Hegel – and ponderous articles by Albert Aurier stressed the fact – that according to the laws of logic and philosophy Gauguin was in the right.

[1]   No attempt has been made to name all Gauguin's pupils here. Some, like Armand Séguin, associated with him assiduously in Brittany. Others only came under his influence as transmitted by Sérusier: one such was Jan Verkade, who turned from Synthetism to religious art and became one of the most remarkable artists of the Beuron school. In the case of Vuillard, the crisis set up by Gauguin's ideas was of short duration: yet he owes to Gauguin the solidity of the system of patches of colour underlying the intense and delicate charm of his compositions. As for A. Maillol, I doubt whether he ever met Gauguin: and yet this Grecian of '*la belle époque*' may have learnt much from the *xoana* of the master of Pont-Aven! (Author's note.)

[2]   As did his friends Emile Bernard, Filiger, De Hahn, Maufra and Chamaillard, who had some influence on the development of his ideas. Remember, too, that he saw a great deal of van Gogh. (Author's note.)

Maurice Denis

The Symbolist Era

Maurice Denis was in his middle sixties when he looked back on the Symbolist moment (in the Gazette des Beaux-Arts, *March 1934). That moment was much out of favour at the beginning of the 1930s, and Denis was understandably somewhat on the defensive in his survey of a period which in 1934 found few to defend it.*

The name 'Impressionism' was in fact never accepted by the artists to whom it refers, but it has the great advantage of being universally recognized and in current use. This is not the case with the term 'Symbolism', which was applied, with equal inaccuracy, to a certain period of modern painting but is now rarely or never either used or understood. At the time when Gauguin, at Le Pouldu, wrote on an earthenware pot the ironical inscription *Sintaize*, the name 'Synthetism' seemed likely to prevail. The term 'Neo-Traditionalism', which I suggested in my first article in *Art et critique* in 1890, was symmetrically contrasted with 'Neo-Impressionism'. It implied that although our ideas were quite new we were returning to a tradition; later, speaking of Cézanne, van Gogh and Gauguin, I described our general tendency as 'directed towards a new classical order'. In any case, and whatever name posterity may apply to the artistic movement, and to the decisive moment in the history of modern art, with which I am concerned here, there are a certain number of images which occur to my mind when I remember that period, which was that of my own youth.

The first image I recall is of the Café Volpini, in a deserted or nearly deserted corner of the great fair of 1889 at the Champ de Mars, in the shadow of the newly built Eiffel Tower. Here, from 10 June onwards, were exhibited ninety-six of the first works of the new school of painting, framed in white. Were they art students' jokes, of the kind then being shown at the 'Incohérents' exhibition? The drawing, distorted almost to the point of caricature, and the flat colours, outraged the public. But those who had once experienced the excitement of such works, in the atmosphere of the period, when the popularity of Alexandre Cabanel and Georges Rochegrosse was at its height, and when Manet's fame had not yet spread beyond the limits of a coterie, would thenceforward be immune to surprise at subsequent audacities; the Fauves, fifteen years later, would recall to them, if not the works, at any rate the effect produced by the works of the 'Peintres symbolistes et synthétistes, chez M. Volpini'.

There were seventeen pictures by Gauguin, painted in Brittany, at Arles and in Martinique. There were twenty-three by Emile Bernard. In addition, there were works by Charles Laval, Emile Anquetin, Emile Schuffenecker, Louis Roy, Daniel de Monfreid, Léon Fauché and, under the pseudonym Ludovic Nemo, Bernard again.

I was still at the Académie Julian, although enrolled at the Ecole des Beaux-Arts. The show was first a dazzlement and then a revelation. Instead of windows opening on to nature, like the paintings of the Impressionists, here were heavily decorative surfaces, strongly coloured, the forms outlined with a thick black line, *cloisonnés* (partitioned off) – for the word *cloisonnisme* was also used of these works. So, too, was the word *japonisme*; these unusual paintings reveal the influence of Japanese woodcuts, of twopence-coloured prints and inn-signs, of Romanesque stylization. And we were reminded, too, of Pissarro's peasant scenes, and above all of Puvis de Chavannes, the painter of *The Poor Fisherman*, that forgotten great master, whose enormous influence on late nineteenth-century painting can never be sufficiently stressed.

Another vivid memory is of Père Tanguy's blue-painted shop in the quiet rue Clauzel, on the eve of the Indépendants exhibition. You could hear washerwomen warbling the 'Chanson des blés d'or': *Ah! quand le rossignol viendra chanter encore . . .* ('Ah! when the nightingale returns to sing again'); and the light clatter of occasional cab-horses' hooves in the silence of that somewhat disreputable district. Our pictures were stacked on the pavement, waiting for the barrow which was to transport them to the Pavillon de la Ville de Paris on the Cours-la-Reine. Van Gogh's portrait of Père Tanguy commemorates his kind stubborn face, under a straw hat; inside Tanguy's little shop were Vincent's suns, Cézanne's great still-lifes and landscapes and his portrait of Emperaire, and *The Night-man's Wife*, now lost. There were many Bernards, too, and Vollard was later to buy one of my first pictures here. This was the place to see Cézanne; in fact the only place where his absurd and splendid works were to be seen. They still seemed absurd even to us, for they were too rich to be easily intelligible. The astonishing eccentric worked on in solitude; he was busy revolutionizing the art of his time and of all time. Tanguy spoke of Monsieur Cézanne in tones of mystery. Gauguin and Bernard knew him, but he avoided

Paris. Did he really exist? Wasn't he just a myth? Tanguy, however, knew that Cézanne was the great master, the genius of the new school of painting. He therefore priced his pictures very high, asking up to three hundred francs!

What should I set between the two wings of this triptych, Tanguy's shop and Volpini's café? Should it be the inn at Le Pouldu or the one at Pont-Aven? (For this I rely on Sérusier's recollections.)

Le Pouldu was, as Charles Chassé has remarked, a sort of a French Tahiti for Gauguin; here, lodging with Marie Henry, who later became Mme Mothéré, with his disciples Meyer de Haan, Laval, Sérusier, Filiger and Seguin – to whom one should add Maxime Maufra and Henry Moret who remained faithful to Impressionism – here he assumed the role of leader of a school, although he denied the imputation with the ironical surliness characteristic of the man and of his time. Gauguin arrived at Le Pouldu in the early summer of 1889, at the time of the Volpini exhibition. And throughout his life he retained the happiest memories of his long stay there, and of his hard-working existence enlivened with paradoxes and serious talk.

But I prefer to think of him in 1888 at Pont-Aven, at Mère Gloanec's, when his painting had just begun to change its character, when his personality, with the probable help of certain theories, was finally asserting itself. Pont-Aven, with its mills and its handsome girls, its Bois d'Amour and its river dotted with picturesque rocks (now ruined by industrial buildings), Pont-Aven attracted painters, particularly students from the Académie Julian.

Gauguin had come there in 1886, and then he had gone to Martinique with Laval. He returned in 1888, having brought back from his voyage to the West Indies a number of already advanced works. Bernard turned up next, having walked over from Saint-Briac. He was twenty years old; he brought in a new element: he knew Lautrec, Anquetin and in particular van Gogh, whom he had met at Cormon's studio. He knew all about literary Symbolism. He was a man of cultured and audacious intelligence, eager for anything new. He played an important part in Gauguin's life, first as friend and then as adversary; Roger Marx was to describe 'little Bernard' as the father of Symbolism.

Bernard, then, stayed at Pont-Aven with Gauguin, Sérusier and Chamaillard. Chaimaillard was a lawyer from Quimper, who delighted the whole group with his naive, amateurish painting. The reactionaries had their own corner in the same inn; they included a certain G. de Maupassant, said to be the father of Guy, who was uncompromisingly hostile to the innovators. It was the custom on the hostess's name-day to hang in the dining-room a painting by each of the guests; he sought to disparage Gauguin's painting by telling Mme de Gloanec: 'No, you can't hang that up. He's having you on.' Then Gauguin thought of a subterfuge: he attributed the still-life he had just painted to an inexperienced artist, Bernard's sister, who had come to visit her brother, and signed it 'Madeleine B'.

This was the moment when Gauguin developed to the full the process of simplification he had begun in Martinique; he painted his *Yellow Christ*, and his *Jacob wrestling with the Angel*, and Bernard painted his great Breton scenes, *Buckwheat* and *The Pardon*. The common principle and watchword of the group was to heighten colour and simplify form. And it was at the end of this historic season that Sérusier brought the 'Talisman' to the studios of the Académie Julian in the Faubourg Saint-Denis, where he served as *massier* (student treasurer). The studios were run by Jules Lefebvre and Doucet. The 'Talisman', that small wooden board covered with pure colours assembled in a certain order, which Sérusier had painted under Gauguin's guidance, was for us the token of the new doctrine.

Just as Bernard's studio in his parents' home at Asnières revealed to me the influence of Cézanne even before I had seen Cézanne's paintings at Tanguy's, so did Sérusier convey Gauguin's doctrines to me before I had seen any Gauguins at the Café Volpini. Sérusier, a doctrinaire apostle, made it his duty to systematize the new ideas he had brought back from Pont-Aven. His word carried weight with us. He loved philosophy, particularly the Alexandrians; he took a keen interest in the music of Berlioz and Wagner; he knew enough about mathematics, physics and exegesis to deal with all the subjects we had so much to heart. Moreover, he had won distinction at the Salon for a picture in sombre tones of a weaver working in the dark; all the more reason for believing him when he preached pure colour.

When, the following summer, he had to confront Gauguin with his own theories, born of that first encounter, I received from him a disillusioned letter written at Pont-Aven. But this was followed by an enthusiastic one from Le Pouldu: 'Here I am on this magnificent beach, where I shall spend a fortnight alone with Gauguin undisturbed, free from care and safe from *apéritifs*.' And, a little later: 'I am living with Gauguin and De Haan in the dining-room of an inn which we have decorated ourselves. I am working a little and learning a great deal. What a lot I shall have to tell you when we meet again!' And finally: 'As to collecting together studies by the whole gang and showing them in someone's studio [as had been suggested], and inviting as many people as possible to see them, it's an excellent idea. I can easily manage it this winter, particularly as Gauguin intends to go to Madagascar to work there for several years, taking with him Bernard, who's been practically turned out by his family. Laval has dropped us. Meyer de Haan, the Dutchman, will go back to Holland or else follow Gauguin. So I have in a way become their executor.'

This he in fact became. Gauguin, on leaving for Tahiti (and not for Madagascar), passed on to him his disciple Jan Verkade, a young Dutchman who was later converted to Catholicism and in 1893 became a monk in the abbey of Beuron. Sérusier's influence was chiefly exerted among the Académie Julian set: it was here that he founded the Nabi group, which first comprised Bonnard, Ibels, Ranson and myself, then later other painters unconnected with our studio: René Piot, K.-X. Roussel and Vuillard. It was only later that we made the acquaintance of Aristide Maillol and Félix Vallotton. The Nabis met for a monthly dinner, lavishly seasoned with paradoxical theories, in the *entresol* of a cheap eating-house in the Passage Brady.

The years 1889 to 1895 were a decisive period of work, theorizing and excitement. We had linked up with the literary Symbolists. Lugné-Poe introduced me to Adolphe Retté, and it was through the intermediary of Retté that my first article was published in 1890 in the journal *Art et critique*. The Théâtre d'Art gave, in May 1891, a benefit performance for Verlaine and Gauguin of *Chérubin*, by Charles Morice (who was later to publish Gauguin's *Noa-Noa*), *Les Uns et les autres* by Verlaine, and, most importantly, *L'Intruse*, which won public acclaim for a writer new to Paris, Maeterlinck.

Gauguin left for Tahiti in 1891; he returned in 1893 and set up his studio, painted light chrome-yellow, at 6 rue Vercingétorix. He dressed eccentrically and was invariably accompanied by Annah la Japonaise [Anna la Javanaise]. He exhibited some pictures at Durand-Ruel's, and in 1895 held a public sale at which Degas bought two paintings. He had become famous. Then he left, never to return.

Gauguin's glory was reflected on his disciples. We exhibited. We painted scenery for Paul Fort's Théâtre d'Art and Lugné-Poe's Théâtre de l'Œuvre. And what scenery, and for what plays! From Ibsen and Maeterlinck to Jarry's *Ubu roi*, a whole series of discoveries and revelations. The art of stage design was transformed, too: *trompe-l'œil* and representational realism were done away with and replaced by imaginative settings, like a tapestried dream-world.

Odilon Redon, who was known through his admirable lithographs, had made friends with the Gauguin group, to which he introduced an element of esoteric mysticism. He entertained us in his flat in the avenue de Wagram with a dignity comparable to that of Mallarmé in the rue de Rome. He was in fact the Mallarmé of painting. His statements seemed to us to issue from the depths. His apocalyptic imagination was concealed behind the affable mask of a perfect man of the world. At this time Gustave Moreau was appointed *chef d'atelier* at the Ecole des Beaux-Arts. René Piot, who had also rebelled against official teaching, returned to the Ecole as Moreau's pupil. Now Moreau was in certain respects at a far remove from our ideas, but he stood for idealism, together with an unusual talent and an intellectual fervour which were to find expression in his teaching and to foster a brilliant line of young painters.

I must also recall, at the risk of surprising certain prejudiced minds, that Edouard Vuillard and I used to go and admire the recent decorations of Albert Besnard at the Ecole de Pharmacie. They offered us a new conception of decorative art, a thrill of modernity. This did not, however, interfere with our passion for Puvis de Chavannes.

What underlay the theories of Sérusier, derived as they were from the ideas of Gauguin and Bernard and, I should add, of Odilon Redon? I have discussed these more fully in my books. Let me merely recall the theory of the two kinds of distortion which in our minds summed up this doctrine: objective distortion, based on a purely aesthetic and decorative idea, on technical principles of colour and composition; and subjective distortion, which involved the personal sensations of the artist, his soul, his poetic vision, but also a certain feeling for nature which excluded, at least in theory, abstraction and 'literature'.

Writers like Charles Morice and Albert Aurier stressed meanwhile the mystico-literary point of view. In an article by Aurier we read that 'the form, the body of any object is the tangible modality of its being, that is to say the visible indication of a thought'; and elsewhere: 'In short, any object in nature is an idea made manifest.' He spoke of a mysterious language, an expressive set of symbols, which linked the art of Gauguin to that of Leonardo da Vinci, Gustave Moreau, Puvis and the Pre-Raphaelites; and he spoke pityingly of 'poor Seurat and his intrinsically sterile learning'. However, this article was illustrated; and the reproductions of a *Street Scene* by Bonnard and a *Woman Mending* by Vuillard made it clear that Aurier's Platonistic formulae did not exactly suit artists who were too much in love with painting, too eager for direct sensations, to settle down in the realm of 'the spiritual and the intangible'.

Meanwhile Bernard had been on his travels, and he became aware of the technical inadequacies of his early manner. After a sojourn in Egypt, his ideas and his painting evolved in an unmistakably and indeed narrowly classical direction. In 1903 he published *La Rénovation esthétique*, in which, as aesthetician, as poet and as painter, he took the exactly opposite view from his Pont-Aven theories.

He had published the letters of van Gogh, who had died in 1890, and had done much to further the fame of Cézanne. He was himself a remarkable artist. But his admiration for the great Venetians prevented him from doing justice either to Cézanne's intuitive classicism or to the exacerbated Romanticism of van Gogh.

Anquetin became absorbed in the study of anatomy and in the scientific aspect of painting. He was quite justified in deploring the ignorance of the younger generation, which had none of the technical instruction formerly given in the studios. Professional skill and the little tricks of the trade are now generally despised, but they are an essential prerequisite for a masterpiece. It is they that provide its fine patina and ensure its preservation. But little by little the life went out of Anquetin's work and he merely went on repeating time-honoured formulae.

Toulouse-Lautrec's great talent produced works of biting realism and developed in the direction of cruelly observant draughtsmanship. The influence of 1890 can be traced only in his engravings and posters; the use of flat colour in unconventional arabesques recalls the highly original decorative compositions of our friend Paul Ranson, founder of the art school which bore his name and incidentally proved a very lively centre for the diffusion and popularization of our theories.

The case of Edouard Vuillard is more complex than that of Lautrec. So rich a personality, such exceptional and varied gifts, cannot easily be fitted into the framework of a definition or of a school. Yet it is undeniable that Vuillard owed a great deal to the Nabis: that art of transposing sensation into the field of decoration, that control of sensation, that strict mastery of his medium, which were the acquired virtues or qualities of this extraordinarily sensitive temperament. From his earliest *Interiors* Vuillard had displayed a lucid and ever-watchful awareness; this acquired an intellectual stiffening from the theories of 1890, which contributed to the full expression of his genius. The 'gourmand turned ascetic', as Jacques Blanche described him, had proved by experience that intelligence and self-mastery are eminently favourable to the perfecting of a body of work founded on immediate sensation, and to the development of a complete painter.

Roussel, a painter of subtle landscapes and of mythological scenes, and a splendid decorator, could likewise, I assume, have no regrets at having absorbed, after some reluctance, the somewhat over-simple formulae of our youthful days.

But Bonnard is the supreme example of a painter who remained faithful to his first aesthetic attitude. His latest works are justly praised for their enduring youthfulness. This is due to the way he re-creates every scene, every object, with an ever-fresh mind, dreaming yet fully awake, and obeying his dream, overthrowing accepted values, replacing natural logics by a logic of his own, into which he brings the irony or tenderness of his vision of the world and his wonder at it. If we compare him with other artists endowed with a magic gift for colour, M. Matisse for example, we are struck by all that lies beneath the surface in Bonnard's painting. Every element in his pictures is charged with psychological significance. He unconsciously practises both sorts of distortion, objective and subjective. . . .

The weakest element in Symbolism was the one which literary Symbolists flaunted: the abuse of odd metaphors, of medieval stereotypes, of obscurity, and of the meretricious pseudo-mysticism dear to certain poets and to the Rosicrucians (whose gatherings we attended with considerable misgivings). All this was soon to pass out of fashion. Yet that state of mind did produce one masterpiece equal to the greatest: *Pelléas et Mélisande*. Meanwhile some of us, beneath all this make-believe, primitivism, mannerism and undirected mysticism, had felt the pull of great spiritual subjects: we turned towards religious art. Circumstances were on our side: a renewal of Christian faith, marked by certain startling conversions, to begin with, and then the opportunity to build or rebuild and decorate new churches. I have said elsewhere how the theories of 1890 seemed to me to favour the renewal of sacred art. It is not for me to insist on this: I have been too much involved with this offshoot of Symbolism to criticize or praise it here. Let me only point out that it was in what has been called the renaissance of religious art that the theories of 1890 found their fullest collective expression.

Lugné-Poe

28 Rue Pigalle

The first volume, Le Sot du tremplin *(Paris 1931), of Lugné-Poe's autobiography is primarily for the theatre enthusiast; but as Lugné was very scrupulous about giving credit to his painter friends for their participation in his adventures,* Le Sot du tremplin *is invaluable for its account of Vuillard at a particularly tender stage in his career.*

The little studio at 28 rue Pigalle was rented in the first place by Pierre Bonnard. We pooled our resources to keep it. I was one of the first to be in default with my share of the expenses, but we stayed together as a band of brothers for the next fifteen years. Since then, the passage of time and the diversity of our undertakings have combined to keep us apart, but we are as fond of one another as ever we were.

We were four, like the Musketeers, at number 28: Maurice Denis, Edouard Vuillard, Pierre Bonnard and I. It was in that little studio, at the very top of a house on the corner of the rue La Bruyère, that the Neo-Traditionalists came into being, whom Arsène Alexandre was the first to single out, and it was there that Gustave Geffroy came to see us. I had known him since my childhood, when my parents lived at 14 rue Martel, and he was then living in Belleville, not far away. I had shown him Denis's first sketches for *Sagesse* and Vuillard's studies of Félicien Mallet in *L'Enfant prodigue.* It was also from number 28 that I bore off to *Art et critique* Maurice Denis's manifesto, which can fairly be called historic, on behalf of the Neo-Traditionalists.

Sérusier, Percheron, Gauguin, Coquelin *cadet,* Ibels, Ranson, Le Barc de Boutteville senior, Camille Mauclair and many others whose names escape me, sat round with us in that studio, which was no bigger than a pocket handkerchief. Its windows looked out on the rue Pigalle. It was the birthplace, also, of the Nabis, those chaste prophets of painting who stood out like a new branch from the proud tree of Signac, Seurat and Pissarro.

Maurice Denis has brought all this out most admirably in *Théories.* While my friends painted away, I bored them to distraction as I went over my parts for the Conservatoire or gave lessons then and there, in front of them. As I had not yet found a theatre of my own, and as I was disgusted by the underhand ways of the Théâtre Libre, I had to fall back on our little studio for my managerial débuts.

April 1891 is marked down in my diary as the month of *The Wild Duck* at the Théâtre Libre. What a touching evening! And what a service it rendered us all!

The Dockers   *c.* 1890

How many a Gregers Werle lives amongst us! Who has not got something of Gregers Werle in him? Who has not in some respect – though it's terrible to say it – got a little of Hjalmar in him? Which of us has not harboured a 'wild duck' in his time?

It was during the previous year that Antoine introduced the wolf into the sheep-fold of Naturalism by putting on Ibsen's *Ghosts*. Zola himself, the great Zola, had recommended the play to Antoine. Antoine had had a presentiment of Ibsen's symbolism, but he didn't know where to look for it. He looked elsewhere, and didn't have the guts to tackle the thing head-on. He'd have had to get away from the gang of parasites who hid the truth from him, wrapped him in cotton wool, told him that he was the rarest of birds, the phoenix, and generally let him get above himself. At the beginning of 1891 Octave Mirbeau had lit the torch for Maeterlinck's *La Princesse Maleine*, and we had all hoped that Antoine would go forward with us. But he did all he could to evade the issue. . . . I couldn't make out what he was up to, but I knew after *La Princesse Maleine* that the theatre held me in thrall again, as it had in the beginning, and that Maeterlinck was destined to personify all our hopes.

It was the poetic aspect of the theatre that needed all our energies. Its poetry had to be as much a matter of decoration as of drama. All the rest was stagey trash, not to be bothered with for a moment. My ideas hardened, and my will with them, until I could think of nothing else. The theatre was a means, also, of helping my painter friends in their early and difficult days. It was from our little studio, which cost us just four hundred francs a year, that their first canvases went out into the world.

I didn't at all mind hawking their pictures round the town. I got Coquelin *cadet* to buy a Denis, though he really preferred Cazin and Rochegrosse. One day I showed him a ravishing Bonnard, for which Bonnard wanted seventy-five francs, a *Woman with Cat*, a mass of interlacing green lines, an enchantment of touches of pale pink, which Bonnard later turned into one panel of a well-known decoration. Coquelin had said 'Try to get me something of that fellow Bonnard's' – pronouncing the name in quite a special way, a smiling good-natured way that was not quite disdainful. 'That fellow Bonnard!' That young madcap, he meant. Well, that little painting was an aristocratic jewel: all poetry, all colour and so full of light that as I took it across Paris I was carried away by my feelings and hoped that it would be snapped up on the spot.

Coquelin looked at it for a long time, turned it round, looked at it again, and then said 'I'd prefer something by that brute of an Ibels – you know, one of those athletes weight-lifting, or a woman with a big behind.' Why did he speak of 'that brute of an Ibels'? I never found out. Ibels will forgive me, I know, if I tell this story forty years later, for there was never anything in the least brutish about him. . . .

Anyway, I went off down the stairs with the Bonnard under my arm. I was mortified, cut to the heart. I had been so confident that Coquelin would buy the painting that I had allowed Bonnard to feel that the sale was as good as made. What if he had already spent the seventy-five francs? I didn't know what to do. Luckily, as I was going home with my tail between my legs, I met a relation of mine. I touched him for the sum in question, went home, hid the painting in the concierge's lodge, and later, under cover of night, got it up into my room.

One of Denis's *Catholic Mysteries* went to Coquelin, and another to Jules Claretie. And I managed to place several Vuillards in the dressing-rooms of illustrious

II **The Landing, rue de Miromesnil 1891**

members of the Comédie Française. . . . It was mainly for my services as an intermediary that I was prized by my three painter friends. But I believed wholeheartedly in them, and in their ability to make light and colour and thought sing out. They gave me new things to think about, and they taught me to look beyond the Conservatoire – and, above all, beyond the Théâtre Libre. It was at the Théâtre Libre, far more than in the army, that I had had my baptism of fire; but there was an absolute lack of imagination about the Théâtre Libre that I found quite stultifying. With my painter friends I found new books to read, a new way of life, and a lively companionship that made me discard my former loves. We read Rimbaud, we read Gide (then at the outset of his career), we read Verlaine, and we read Maeterlinck and Ibsen. . . .

And now I'd like to describe my three friends.

Maurice Denis, to begin with. He and I had never lost contact with one another. Ever since we were together in the drawing-class at the Lycée Condorcet I had admired his quiet, contained intelligence. His eyes proved him to be a visionary, a lover of the beauty of pure line; his brow stood for order and lucidity. At school he had been a friend of Gabriel Trarieux and of Marcel Proust; we all saw him as a paragon of intelligence and application. Poet and painter in one, he relied on reason and tranquillity to keep his instincts in check. We were amazed by this faculty of his, and attributed it to the turn of mind which led him, throughout his life, to a steadfast belief in God. Yet there was in his eyes, and in his way of looking at the world, something that ran counter to it all; thought and execution were from time to time – or so we supposed – at war with one another. His friends were not all as mystical as he; but at number 28 each of us respected the others' natures.

Vuillard I had come to know through Denis. He was very different in character. Fastidious by nature, he was exempt from the fanaticism which underlay Denis's gentle ways. In Vuillard's company, life smiled and took on its most peaceful aspect. Nothing could have been more harmonious than Vuillard's way of life and his behaviour in society. He was loving-kindness personified. Never the man to put himself forward, he effaced himself behind the merits of his three colleagues. I got the Théâtre Libre to agree that he should design one of their programmes. I tried to do the same for Bonnard, but failed; I still have Bonnard's design.

Bonnard was the humorist among us. His nonchalant gaiety and spontaneous wit came out strongly in his paintings at that time. They were decorative in intention, but there was a satirical element in them which he was to abandon later. The reader will perhaps remember his poster for France-Champagne, and, above all, his illustrations for the *Méthode de Solfège Illustré*, a marvel of wit and invention which would put fresh heart into any child who had to struggle with Claude Terrasse's rather cheerless music-primer.

Bonnard was not at all like either Vuillard or Denis. Yet all three of them stood on the threshold of life with a nobility of ambition that did me an enormous amount of good. Bonnard in particular was a continual source of energy and excitement for me, so imaginative was he in his use of line and colour, and so graceful and good-humoured in the way he set out his ideas. A conversation at number 28 would put the whole world in perspective for me. A turning-point in my life was at hand – thanks to Darzens, who translated *Ghosts* for Antoine, shook the Théâtre Libre from top to bottom, and quite involuntarily made me all the more determined to bring my Théâtre de l'Œuvre into being. The four of us went to *Ghosts*, as we had been together to *The Wild Duck*, and we felt that that great poet, Ibsen, was going to change our whole way of seeing the world. All Europe was taxing him at that time with 'symbolism', but we felt that his naturalism was leading elsewhere.

It was also at number 28 that I got to know the large-hearted Paul Sérusier, most resourceful and devoted of the Nabis. He was in a way our director of programmes at the Œuvre, just as he was our director of décors. Those décors remain as a monument to the first phase of our activity; I must add that Vuillard was the best of advisers, where the theatre was concerned, and one who dedicated himself to it wholeheartedly from the first moment of its inception. He often came with me to classes at the Conservatoire.

Dom Willibrod Verkade

Some Recollections of the Nabis

Jan Verkade was close to the Nabis before entering the Church, and his Le Tourment de Dieu: Etapes d'un moine peintre *(1924) gives a vivid first-hand account of their circle.*

One day Sérusier said to me: 'Let's go and see the Nabi, Denis, at Saint-Germain; you don't know him yet.' 'What sort of a painter is he?' I asked. 'You'll see,' said Sérusier; 'Denis is a true Symbolist.' The country round Paris is as beautiful a landscape as I have ever seen. The neighbourhood of the charming little town of Saint-Germain-en-Laye reminds one of Italy, particularly of Tuscany, except that its colours are even richer and more glowing.

About three o'clock in the afternoon we knocked at the door of Maurice Denis's studio. It was opened by the Nabi himself, a young man barely twenty years old. He was of medium height. A new beard framed his round rosy cheeks; thick dark brown hair hung down over his fine brow, beneath which his eyes shone brightly. There was a virginal purity and a child-like gentleness about his gaze. He was like a young girl who has never left her mother's side, and his paintings gave the same impression. It is true that they were the work of a very young man, but they already showed great maturity. They bore the mark of a rich, chaste and candid imagination, and displayed a highly developed sense of colour. There were among them a number of religious pictures which radiated that happy piety displayed by Catholic children at their first communion.

By the side of this strangely gifted young man I felt myself very small. I have seldom been so profoundly conscious of the fragmentary and superficial nature of my education. I felt instinctively how greatly his faith had enriched this young artist who, as Sérusier told me, had grown up an ardent Catholic and while still very young had passed his *baccalauréat* with high marks in philosophy. We spent a long while looking at Denis's paintings, then we went for a walk in the neighbourhood of the little town. It was a wonderful day in early spring, at that time when the buds are swelling on the trees but have not yet opened, when the mossy trunks rise up from the copper-coloured soil and branches and twigs glow blood-red against the blue sky. Nature is full of promise then, telling of its future blossoming.

And it seemed to harmonize with the painting of that high-souled young man, Nabi Denis, whose works, too, foretold an imminent springtide, resplendent with blossom. As we walked we often recognized elements of landscape which the young artist had introduced, with felicitous effect, into his paintings.

As day drew to a close the colours of trees and soil glowed ever more brightly. The Seine wound like a gleaming blue-green ribbon between dark orange hillsides, and in the mysterious shadow of a small wood the last rays of the setting sun gleamed on a few slender trees. We can never forget our first introduction to whatever great boons life has bestowed upon us. And so it was with that day to which I owe one of my dearest friends.

As I have said, every Saturday afternoon the group of Nabis (Nebiim would be a more correct plural) met in the studio of the painter Paul Ranson. He had been married for several years at the time when I made his acquaintance. His wife, a charming, merry Frenchwoman, welcomed her guests with delightful informality and gave them beer and sandwiches. Among the regular visitors to these gatherings was Nabi Paul Sérusier, a thickset young man with long fair hair and auburn beard. He was more Scandinavian than French in appearance, and reminded one of the cheerful drinker in Manet's painting *Le bon bock*. Ranson, who had given all the Nabis appropriate nicknames, called him 'the Nabi with the glowing beard'. I myself was christened 'the obeliscal Nabi'.

Another regular visitor was Edouard Vuillard. He was a true Frenchman of the same stamp as St Francis de Sales, whom he closely resembled. His was a deeply sensitive and tactful nature. He never asserted anything dogmatically, for fear of not speaking the truth. We loved his witty sayings, and we listened with pleasure to his conversation, which awakened in us all sorts of new ideas. Vuillard's friend Pierre Bonnard was nicknamed the 'Japanizing Nabi' because his paintings at that time were influenced by Japanese art; he used to come regularly to our gatherings. He was prodigiously gifted, but too judicious to display his superiority; he knew how to conceal the element of genius in himself behind a sort of boyish playfulness. Like Vuillard, he preferred to work intuitively, wielding the brush with passion, under remote control by thought and will. He was wholly unconcerned with personal advancement. He had a profound aversion for whatever in art is due to mere manual dexterity and consequently fails to move us. It is true that his paintings, like those of the other Nabis, were often felicitous improvisations rather than finished works. But none the less they are among the finest things produced by French art during the past thirty years.

I must next mention Nabi Ker-Xavier Roussel, who was akin to Vuillard and Bonnard in mind and in tendency. He was the son of a well-known Parisian doctor. He had a considerable aptitude for classical form and composition; one might describe him as an Impressionist Claude Lorrain. Unfortunately his delicate health often prevented him from obeying the natural ardour of his temperament. He was frequently obliged to lay down his brush, but he would then turn to charcoal or pastel, handling both of these with masterly ease.

Maurice Denis, the 'Nabi aux belles icônes', could not regularly attend the Nabis' meetings since, as I have said, he lived at Saint-Germain. But it was always a great delight for us when he came. Denis was the friendliest of creatures. And this was why we were all so happy about his early success. Almost always when Denis was among his friends, his serious and religious turn of mind brought the conversation round to philosophical questions. I took no part in these, for I 'didn't want to think about such things till later on'.

Ranson, our host, was a witty southerner; his father, a former deputy, was a Protestant and he himself a theosophist. His painting, although akin to the modern Symbolist movement in its subject-matter, was technically closer to the official academic style. For this reason he was less successful than the other Nabis, which often discouraged the good fellow. Like almost all Frenchmen, he wrote very well. I have some letters from him, of real literary merit, which express the profound admiration and affection he bore his friends. Unfortunately he died young.

These six young men; Sérusier, Denis, Vuillard, Bonnard, Roussel and Ranson, formed the nucleus of the little group, which also comprised a few other members. I should like to mention in particular Nabi Pierre Hermant, a musician of whom I shall speak later, and Nabi Henri Cazalis, to whom Ranson had given the charming nickname of 'Ben Callyre Cazalis', because he had studied Orientalism for a few months. Cazalis had already embarked on a number of careers, but had abandoned them one after the other. There was one point, however, on which he proved unshakable; and that was friendship. . . .

I cannot better describe what these gatherings meant to us Nabis than by quoting the words in which St Augustine spoke of the friends who surrounded him at Carthage in his youth:

'All kinds of things rejoiced my soul in their company – to talk and laugh and do each other kindnesses; read pleasant books together, pass from light jesting to talk of the deepest things and back again; differ without rancour, as a man might differ from himself, and when most rarely dissension arose find our normal agreement all the sweeter for it; teach each other or learn from each other; be impatient for the return of the absent, and welcome them with joy on their homecoming; these and such like things, proceeding from our hearts as we gave affection and received it back, and shown by face, by voice, by the eye, and a thousand other pleasing ways, kindled a flame which fused our very souls and of many made us one' (*Confessions*, IV, 8, tr. F.J. Sheed).

Back in Paris, I rented a room in a hotel in the rue de Richelieu, close to the Théâtre Français. The greatest event of my first weeks was the opening of the Salon des Indépendants. The most original and interesting work shown, apart from that of the Neo-Impressionists, was that of the Nabi group, led by Sérusier, Denis, Bonnard and Vuillard. I showed a few paintings myself: the critics always mentioned me in the same breath as my friends. I then enjoyed the first modest success of my life. The weeks that followed were devoted to preparing for a performance of Maeterlinck's *Seven Princesses*, which was to be given on Palm Sunday at the home of a privy councillor. It was acted by little puppets; the play was read by Sérusier, his brother and the daughter of the conductor Lamoureux. Sérusier and Vuillard had made the scenery for the tiny stage, and I had painted the curtain. As the councillor lived out at Passy, preparations and rehearsals took up a great deal of time. But the performance was highly successful, and gave us Nabis a chance to frequent other social circles. Everyone was amazed that with such limited means we had produced so poignant a dramatic effect.

The Nabis' traditional gatherings at Ranson's studio on Saturday afternoons were as gay and stimulating as ever, and so were the evening parties given by another

Nabi, Hermant the musician, who played Bach and Wagner to his friends on a great harmonium. He lived next door to the painter Meissonier, for whom we had scant respect. In the evenings, when we left to go home, we never failed to display our contempt for the *prince des pompiers*, the supreme stuffed shirt. We behaved so outrageously that one evening we had a set-to with a policeman, who wanted to take one of us to the station. As we all insisted on accompanying him, the policeman soon let us go, saying severely: 'Gentlemen, behave properly next time.' He had probably noticed us on many previous occasions.

And so every day brought some new distraction: regular visits to a merchant friend of my father's, where I took dancing lessons; introductions to various social circles; dates and parties; innumerable occupations which undoubtedly contributed to my education but which entailed the sacrifice of my real work.

Romain Coolus

Edouard Vuillard

Romain Coolus contributed to the Mercure de France *for 1 January 1934 an article on Vuillard which is, for much of its length, a piece of indigestible philosophizing. The exordium, reprinted here, is on the other hand of great interest for its exploration of a side of Vuillard's nature which few of his friends had the opportunity to penetrate.*

Vuillard is one of the most significant artists of our time; but to those who have only a passing acquaintance with him he must seem a most problematical person. The way he looks and the things he says do not tell us much about his nature, his character or his cast of mind. Most people give up the struggle to understand him, and from their first social contacts with him little remains but an immediate attraction. Vuillard is the most secret of men; and if he has disconcerted many of his interlocutors – many of his admirers, even – this would not surprise him, for he has often disconcerted himself also.

If I went so far as to call him 'enigmatic', he would take it as an affront to his modesty. If he is mysterious, none the less, it is because all men are mysterious – above all, those in whom nature has implanted the cruel gift of creativity. But, even among artists, there are some who feel an imperious need to externalize, to explain themselves, to trust to words – insufficient or misleading as these may be – to spell out their ambitions, their tastes and their preferences. Like sailors who have to subordinate a love of adventure to the most precise mathematical calculations, they chart their passage across the inward sea on which they cope with the currents of the unconscious and its treacherous patches of fog.

Vuillard never unburdens himself in this way. He never craves the company of complaisant henchmen. Never will you find him in eruption on matters confidential. There are playwrights who, when at work on an idea that has not assumed its final shape, will buttonhole the first person they see and pour out the whole story in the hope that it will clarify itself. Vuillard is not at all like that: expedients of that sort are not for him. If the impossible ever happened, and he were tempted to reveal himself in a sudden impulse of expansiveness, two things would hold him back: modesty, and the habit of thinking twice.

Like most men who have an intense inner life, Vuillard has an almost physical horror of speaking about himself. It grieves him to think, however far ahead of the event, of the astonishment with which his interlocutor would receive confidences necessarily severed from all the psychological antecedents which conditioned them, on the one hand, and would explain them, on the other.

Quite apart from that, his intellectual probity is such that any positive statement about himself would seem to him quite reckless. True or false? He would find it hard to say. His is a watchful and a reflective nature; he never expresses an opinion without having thought it over at length and with great concentration. For this reason people who have spoken with him only briefly go away with the idea that he is over-discreet and wrapped up in his thoughts. They may have been struck, occasionally, by an unexpected insight that Vuillard has expressed in strikingly apt terms. They may even have suspected that his timidity is sometimes a mask for violences kept well under control. They may have glimpsed the treasure-house of ideas which Vuillard has striven to drag forth from the shadows of his discretion, but they will end, none the less, by attributing a sibylline quality to Vuillard's wariness with words; and they will be disconcerted by a personality which is incurably hostile to any form of conversation that could lead to self-aggrandizement.

I myself had the good fortune to meet Vuillard at the very beginning of my career, in 1891, at the time of *La Revue Blanche* and the Théâtre de l'Œuvre. We have been curious about one another, if I may so put it, ever since. The exigences of our respective professions have not allowed us to meet as often as we might have wished; but thanks to certain friends of both of us, who invited us to spend part of our summers beneath the same roof, we came in time to know one another really well. Ambling round the countryside, talking at our ease by the fire, we had every opportunity of exchanging ideas. (I remember especially an autumn in Burgundy when we managed to keep away from Paris until Christmas.) This must be my excuse if, in the course of this essay, I attribute certain opinions to Vuillard. I say 'attribute' because, with anyone as haunted by anxiety as is Vuillard, one can never be quite sure that one will not misrepresent him. I may be arbitrary, I may even be misleading, in what I say: for errors of that kind I offer my apologies in advance.

Vuillard comes originally from the Jura. He bears the marks of that ancient French province – not least in his powers of concentration. The men of the Jura talk little. They do not live out their lives in the market-square, and 'public life', in its wider sense, does not attract them as it attracts the voluble, disputatious men of the south. Nor have they that rough gaiety, that passion for deals done in the open, which one can find in Normandy. Nor, finally, have they the fundamental melancholy, that misted-over sadness, which characterizes the Breton spirit. The people of the Jura are as remote from a boisterous optimism, at one extreme, as they are from a resignation which accepts the worst, on the other. They just have an inherited disposition to take life seriously, to think very carefully before taking any decision, and never to improvise, either in daily life or in their professional activity. I have often been struck by the importance which Vuillard attached to the word 'importance'. Considerations which the scepticism of the Parisian would have rejected as pointless or secondary were treated by Vuillard in quite a different spirit: he would think them over at length, look deeply into their origins, and set himself to foresee their consequences.

Given this turn of mind, it was natural that when Vuillard felt in himself a vocation for painting he examined the whole matter with the utmost care before accepting it as a reality. If he had such an exceptional gift, what did it mean? Where would it lead him, and should he follow it? Those were the questions he asked himself.

His education had equipped him to undertake an inquiry of this kind, which was as much moral as psychological in its implications. His native province had endowed him with a natural earnestness. He had been brought up in the strictest bourgeois tradition. A stern religious education completed the traditional picture. Devotional problems beset him at a very early age; he had an artist's nature, and both his intelligence and his sensitivity reacted strongly to the problems in question. That intelligence and that sensitivity were often at odds with one another, as we can see over and over again in his work; their lifelong opposition is in fact one of that work's most evident characteristics, and it was present from the beginning.

Vuillard was deeply marked by his early education. Among painters of modern life none is more sophisticated – more voluptuous, some would say; yet there is something paradoxically religious about him. It is not just that he has always lived in a way that is sober and dignified to the point, almost, of austerity. The apartment in which he lives, the studio in which he works, have always had something monastic about them. One has only to watch him, as he prepares his colours à la colle on a little stove and in the humblest of saucepans, to realize that he is no more concerned with the outward surroundings in which his spiritual activity goes forward than were the artisans of the Middle Ages or the God-fearing painters of the Renaissance who worked in the service of the Church.

I think I am pretty safe in saying that from his adolescence every day of Vuillard's life has presented itself to him in the rainbow-light of a moral predicament. This predicament extends into every department of his life: in each, a choice has to be made, whether in art, in friendship, in business, or in the day-to-day traffic of society. In spite of himself, the old, long-instilled habit of religious examination still dominates his everyday life. It has been laicized into philosophical meditation, but it is still there. His state of mind is the exact opposite of the frivolity and irresponsibility of most of our contemporaries. Vuillard takes everything to heart.

His inner life has never, in fact, ceased to be dramatic in the true sense of the word. His consciousness is a theatre of conflict, as I said earlier, between his intelligence and his sensibility. If he had lived apart from the world, in Trappist style, I do not doubt that he would have ended as a Jansenist. I can imagine him imposing upon himself a life of conventual severity. His principles would have led to moral doctrines as implacable in their intransigence as those of Rance. But his vocation led him eventually to a secular form of art, whose first aim is to capture the attention of the observer and seduce him with sensual delights. It therefore came about that his principles had to give way somewhat in order to accommodate themselves to the weaknesses (often beguiling enough) of human nature. This kind of accommodation is characteristic of the Society of Jesus, and it is doubtless in this sense that we must understand Vuillard when he smilingly describes himself as 'jesuitical'. The Jansenist is systematically hostile to every divergence from the disciplines that lead to salvation. Deliberately he exiles himself from the world, and, like Pascal, relegates painting to the category of despicable vanities. The Jesuit by contrast

I An Outspoken Dinner Party *c.* 1891

IV Lilacs 1892

The Lady in Blue   *c.* 1894

remains a member of society, does his best to find subtle vindications for human behaviour, and makes a plausible case for the legitimization of the painter's vocation. The painter's ardours are devoted, before all things, to the procurement for the senses of satisfactions hitherto unknown.

In this way, and at the outset of his career, Vuillard certainly had to justify his art to himself. His admirers can only rejoice that he came out on the side of the Jesuits and against Pascal.

Paul Signac

A Visit to Vuillard, 1898

Signac's was a genial, forthright, rumbustious nature. He liked to argue things out in the open, and it disappointed him very much when he failed to carry the day. The extract from his diaries which is reprinted here is one of many which make us impatient for their complete publication. It was first edited by John Rewald, in La Gazette des Beaux-Arts *(April 1952).*

Vuillard took me to his home. He's a sensitive and intelligent person and a highly strung, questioning painter. You feel that he has an unresting passion for art. His way of life has a dignity that commands respect. He lives with his mother, keeps well away from the cliques, and does his work in their small family apartment. He showed me sketches from every phase of his evolution. His deftly noted interiors have great charm. He has a marvellous understanding of the timbre of things. They're the work of a fine painter – those many-coloured panels, predominantly dark in key, but always with an explosion of bright colour that somewhere re-establishes the harmony of the whole picture. The contrast of tone, the skilfully achieved chiaroscuro – these balance a scheme of colour which, though often grey and languid in effect, is always unusual and delicate – almost unhealthily so, in fact.

Of course Vuillard, as a painter, has freed himself completely from that reality with which we others have to contend. Every artist must take his inspiration, to a certain extent, direct from nature; Vuillard balances too far on the side of fantasy, whereas our group is committed to reality. So strong, in his work, is the element of fantasy that he has to keep these little panels: it would be practically impossible for him to go further. The people in his pictures are not properly defined. As he's an admirable draughtsman it must be that he just *doesn't want* to give them mouths and hands and feet. His finished pictures are like sketches. If he had to work on a big scale he'd have to be more exact – and what would become of him then? *We* put in too much detail; and he, as it seems to me, not enough. It's a real dilemma, and well we know it.

I was very pleased to have visited this delightful man – and pleased, too, with the confidence which led him to reveal to me all the secrets of his art. It did me a great deal of good to discover that Vuillard, though his means are as different as possible from ours, is engaged in the same search for art and involved, like ourselves, in the cruel dilemmas of representation.

▲ VI   The Salon with Three Lamps, rue Saint-Florentin   1899

◀ VII   Mother and Child   *c.* 1899

André Gide

A Walk Round the Salon d'Automne, 1905

For some years Gide was a close friend of Maurice Denis, and in this way he came to have an intimate knowledge of the ambitions of Denis, Vuillard, Bonnard and Roussel. The following is taken from an article which Gide published in La Gazette des Beaux-Arts *(1 December 1905).*

To return to M. Vuillard's decorations. I don't know quite what is the most admirable thing about them. Perhaps it is M. Vuillard himself. He is the most personal, the most intimate of story-tellers. I know few pictures which bring the observer so directly into conversation with the artist. I think it must be because his brush never breaks free of the emotion which guides it; the outer world, for Vuillard, is always a pretext, an adjustable means of expression. And above all it's because M. Vuillard speaks almost in a whisper – as is only right, when confidences are being exchanged – and we have to bend over towards him to hear what he says.

There is nothing sentimental or high-falutin' about the discreet melancholy which pervades his work. Its dress is that of everyday. It is tender, and caressing; and if it were not for the mastery that already marks it, I should call it timid. For all his success, I can sense in Vuillard the charm of anxiety and doubt. He never brings forward a colour without making it possible for it to fall back, subtly and delightfully, into the background. Too fastidious for plain statement, he proceeds by insinuation – note, in the two large 'landscapes with figures', the indefinable carmined violet – but with such sureness of touch that the carmine, though it continues to astonish us, seems nevertheless inevitable. He never strives for brilliant effect; harmony of tone is his continual preoccupation; science and intuition play a double role in the disposition of his colours, and each one of them casts new light on its neighbour, and as it were exacts a confession from it.

How should one explain, to those who have no feeling for them, the interest of M. Bonnard's pictures? In their composition wit and even mischief, play a greater part than reason: each canvas, for this reason, has a feeling of novelty and bizarre excitement. Scrutiny and analysis cannot exhaust the aesthetic amusement which they have to offer; this amusement springs from the colour itself, and from the drawing, rather than from some accountable sleight-of-hand. Whether he paints an omnibus, a dog, a cat or a pair of steps, his very touch, quite independently of the subject, is full of irreverent mischief.

Julius Meier-Graefe

Cézanne and the Nabis

Meier-Graefe's pioneering classic, Entwicklungsgeschichte der modernen Kunst, *was first published in German in 1904. The following extract is taken from the English edition,* The Development of Modern Art *(London 1908).*

No member of the school of Cézanne has succeeded in surpassing the master. But, where there is no teacher, it is inaccurate to talk of a school. It was not by spoken words that the seed was sown in this case. Nor is it Cézanne alone who leads the youth of France. Renoir, Fantin and, once again, Delacroix, divide their homage. If I have, nevertheless, spoken of the school of Cézanne in this connection, it is because certain essential aims of the younger men at least reveal the influence of Cézanne, and because this interrelation is the sole bond of union between a number of very dissimilar painters. [Vuillard, Bonnard and Roussel] should not be grouped with Denis, Vallotton and Gauguin's circle, to whom their relation is but super-ficial; they should be considered quite apart from this society. It is true that like these, they started from synthesis, and claimed at first to be purely decorative artists; each of them worked as an ornamentist, and even as an industrial artist. But this reaction with them was but a recoil, enabling them to rush forward more impetuously on the path of purely pictorial art. They have as a fact, far more in common with those great masters we have called the pillars of modern painting, save that they lack all trace of that element of Courbet which is perceptible in these their predecessors. The animal strain is altogether foreign to their manner. As opposed to it, they might be called 'spirituels'. This gives them the aspect of decadents as compared with the others. And they are in fact decadents, in the same sense as their forerunners, and all modern painters, are decadent more or less; and in a greater degree than the others, their painting lacks the strong support of a clearly defined tendency, and of a teacher. But tradition works in their highly developed instinct, and their taste enables them to profit by it. In their technique, however, they are more remote from the old masters, less methodical even than Renoir, who is said to have once despairingly confided to an acquaintance that he had no notion how to paint, and he was inclined to give up art altogether, as he could not get beyond dilet-tantism – or than Cézanne, whose spleen led him to take his place in a student's class at Aix to learn drawing. All this is less incomprehensible than it sounds. It seems absurd in relation to our admiration for their works; but it seems natural to them in relation to their admiration for the old masters. Their modesty blinds them to the necessary compensations of development.

The old masters utter well-turned phrases; as compared with these, the words of the nineteenth-century leaders sound like suppressed exclamations; the younger men speak in interjections. And yet they echo back to us; that is the marvellous part of it. We may ask ourselves which is the greater miracle – the pictures evolved from the bearish vigour of Courbet, or the harmonies that breathe from the trem-bling essays of these young men.

They are all young still, born about the year 1865, are for the most part of the same age – Vuillard is a year younger than Bonnard and Roussel – and made their début early in the 1890s, when Denis organized a modest exhibition of his own works and those of his friends at Saint-Germain. Parisians made their acquaintance through Le Barc de Boutteville, and afterwards in the exhibitions of Les Indépendants, to which they have remained faithful contributors. They are habitually classed together, because they studied together and developed together. But this development was worked out on very dissimilar lines, diverging more and more with years.

All three bear the same relation to Cézanne as did Fantin-Latour to Delacroix. They are another genus, less grandiose, though no less artistic, of smaller dimensions, showing more sympathy with the large *kakemono* than with the modest engraving. The great simplicity of the elders desired a decisive form of expression, in which there is always something of the combative spirit that drove them to the Salon des Refusés. The younger men are impelled less to fight for watchwords than to collect with all diligence, to enlarge and widen their aims, to keep their eyes on what lies near them, and also on what is far off.

Cézanne was translated into more intimate terms by them. All three retained his mosaic-like technique; it seems, indeed, to have become more deliberate in their hands. The pattern is changed; the stitches are smaller, but at the same time more evident. We see how the thing is done. The mysterious element in Cézanne becomes more comprehensible; the means are used so unerringly that the effect can be demonstrated. There is no genius as yet in the matter, but an extraordinary amount of talent; their technical development affords a parallel to the progress the Neo-Impressionists owed to Monet. Vuillard, the one whose works are most in demand today, remains the still-life painter. He uses human beings in the composition of his still-life pieces, but the fact that they are human beings is not the important thing in the composition. All things seem to serve him merely to enrich his palette. He groups them, and they seem to disappear in the process; in the little interiors he affects we see at first only walls, windows, furniture, curtains and such-like. The figures are hardly necessary, we divine their presence from the surroundings. No artist has ever so suggested the soul of an interior – the sense of habitation. There are people who see in him only the gifted colourist and hieroglyphist, and it is possible that he desires no higher fame himself; the unconscious charm of his art is all the more fascinating for this. We enjoy the same sort of intimacy with him as in conversation with certain agreeable people, when the talk results in a mutual perception of subtle things, when thoughts no longer require words for their interchange, and we are silent lest we should disturb them. We are sometimes reminded of little sketches by Whistler; but when Whistler gives himself up to pleasant intimations, Vuillard begins to paint. There is always something in the background with him. It is possible to have one of his interiors in the house for a month, and one fine day to discover a figure in the corner, and not only a figure, but a whole story. Not a story that can be told in words, be it understood; they are painted corners. His finest and simplest pictures – those which entitle him to rank among the modern decorative masters – are in tempera [*à la colle*].

Pierre Véber

My Friend Vuillard

It was through Pierre Véber that Vuillard first met the Natansons as a schoolboy. Many years later, when Vuillard was elected to the Institut, Véber wrote this little text for Les Nouvelles Littéraires *(30 April 1938).*

Just on fifty-three years ago at the Lycée Condorcet the class in *rhétorique* included two future cabinet ministers and a future emperor. The two future ministers were L. L. Klotz and Joseph Capus, younger brother of the writer. The future emperor of the Sahara was a taciturn young man by the name of Jacques Lebaudy. There were also, in the same class, a future deputy, Louis-Louis Dreyfus, who made his mark in the newspaper world; an eminent laryngologist, Dr Clément; a composer, André Fijan; two playwrights; and three future luminaries of the world of painting, Edouard Vuillard, Maurice Denis and K.-X. Roussel. Providence must really have been looking ahead when those three found themselves in the same school and in the same form.

The friendships formed at that time have lasted for ever, and now Vuillard has joined his old classmate Maurice Denis under the cupola of the Institut.

Vuillard then was much as he is today. He was of medium height, spoke slowly and spoke little, and thought things through with great care, as if to make sure of finding the right words for whatever was on his mind. His voice was soft and gentle, and from time to time he collapsed in brief and guileless laughter. He was quick to grow his sumptuous beard; age has barely whitened it. He was the third child of a most admirable mother who lived in a dark mezzanine above the rue du Marché-Saint-Honoré and kept her family going as a dressmaker. It was there that we used to go and see our friend Vuillard, and we were as fond, almost, of Madame Vuillard as if she had been our own mother. There was something about her that was quite exceptionally pure and noble. She was absolutely devoted to her son, in a way that was marvellous to see. She believed in his vocation; and she devoted herself to it and to him, with a wholeheartedness and forgetfulness of self that I have almost never found elsewhere. It is thanks to her that Vuillard was able to become the artist that he is today; he also owes to his mother the steadfast intelligence, the candour and the integrity which made us seek him out as a friend. It is from her that he inherited the almost implausible modesty which has never left him, even in the face of un-hoped-for successes. Vuillard today is one of the acknowledged masters of modern art; but he has never changed his way of life. All that has happened is that he now gives more and more money away.

Madame Vuillard also passed on to her son a solid and genuine faith in God; he has never lost it. Doubtless it has played a part in his refusal ever to put himself forward; for years he would not let his name be mentioned as a candidate for the Académie des Beaux-Arts, and in the end his friends almost had to force him to stand for election.

His life has passed almost without outward incident. Yet I know few men who have done so much or done it with so much ardour and such fighting spirit. His long career in the service of art has been one unbroken struggle. And yet he cared nothing for money and nothing for 'honours'. I have never heard him say anything that bespoke ambition in any of its forms.

Maurice de Coppet was a close friend of ours. His father was the priest-in-charge at the church of the Oratoire and, as such, an important personage in the Protestant world. Maurice himself did very well in the diplomatic service. He was connected with the Siegfried family, which played a great part in the fortunes of the Third Republic. We were continually together, he, Vuillard, and I, and constantly in and out of one another's houses. Vuillard never said much about his plans for the future. He just wanted to pass his examinations as well as possible.

This achieved, he began to leave us somewhat to our own devices. When school-friends leave school and go their separate ways, a moment of crisis is bound to arise in their relationships. Nor was Vuillard destined for the orthodox road to prosperity. After eighteen months he realized that he had learned nothing of consequence at the Ecole des Beaux-Arts and decided to go his own way. Conscientious in all things, he had done his best to follow the official line. What fired his enthusiasm, he told us, was the meetings of the little group who called themselves the Nabis, or prophets. And they did, after all, deserve the name, for they gave their lives to a mysterious religion, and some of them, in the end, were that religion's victims. They were disinterestedness personified and kept their distance from the Société Nationale and the Société des Artistes Français; such support as they had came directly from picture-dealers and private collectors.

Many a holder of a famous name in the theatre and the arts has found his or her way, since then, to Vuillard's studio above the Place Vintimille. It was there that the emissaries of the Institut sought him out. The Academician's bottle-green uniform with its gold facings is the first and only uniform that Vuillard has ever worn. Perhaps he put it on in part to please the memory of Madame Vuillard, who had set no bounds to her hopes for him. And then, by honouring Vuillard, the Académie has honoured a whole generation. I can hear, from my desk, the guileless little laugh with which he will have greeted the news of his nomination!

Edouard Vuillard

Letter to a Friend

In Arts *(2 April 1948), the following letter from Vuillard to Alfred Natanson was published with an introduction by Denise Mellot, daughter of Alfred Natanson and Marthe Mellot and sister of Annette Vaillant. It is reprinted here, slightly abridged, for the light which it sheds on Vuillard's qualities as a friend.*

To Monsieur A. Natanson, private soldier, 132nd regiment of the line, 8th Company, Rheims.

22 April 1895

My dear Friend

I don't have much confidence in the encouragement I could offer. I could so easily seem brutal and unfeeling and I don't want you to turn against me. Your note – forgive me if I speak of myself – touched me deeply at a moment when *everything* sets my teeth on edge. Everyone, myself included; everything that I do; everything that I say; everything that everyone else does and says. I need to overflow a bit, and yet dare not. Do you know what it is to have had total confidence in everything and everyone and then find that only a very few landmarks are still standing and that one made a great mistake in not realizing that *all things are relative*, and that that is true above all in matters of the heart?

I'm rather downcast, for I had believed entirely in certain forms of behaviour that I now realize do not apply. Fundamentally I'm unchanged, thank Heavens, and I'm not complaining or 'in despair' – but I do feel like a child who no longer knows what's solid and what isn't. There may still be solid things in the world, but I'm not sure what they are.

I got used to abrupt material changes quite early in life – in fact I've nothing more to learn about them – but in the other domain I had no idea that things were as they actually are. I didn't imagine that it would apply to me, in any case. I can't say what it is that helps me to get going again, though I have a very clear notion of it when it happens.

Forgive me for not having anything better to say to you. But there is a certain analogy between our two cases, I think? One simply doesn't know how much one can bear. You'll probably be amazed, in the end, by what you went through and how you got out of it. And you *will* get out of it – one always does. The only thing I can say is – don't brood! Don't hug your wounds! They'll be painful enough already. Talk to your friends about them – it helps a little. As for the idea that you want to get ill again – it's too childish to bother with. You know for yourself that it doesn't make sense.

I'm not doing much – just watching the leaves grow (literally). I did a bit of painting today, and in between I ruminate, clutching at anything that will stave off depression. It works, to my surprise, though I'm always fearing the worst. I expect it'll go on that way for a long while. I shall think of nothing but myself and be amazed to find everyone else doing the same.

Pierre Puvis de Chavannes

A Conversation with Vuillard

From La Renaissance de l'Art Français et des Industries de Luxe *(February 1926), pp. 87–90. The author was the nephew of Puvis the painter.*

Not long ago I found myself talking to Mme Henry Lapauze who told me that she had just had a long conversation about my uncle with Edouard Vuillard. She told me to lose no time in going to see Vuillard and recording his words for posterity.

This is what he told me:

'Every least thing about Manet or Renoir has been noted down – and quite rightly, but with your uncle the case is quite different. Since he died, no one has made a serious attempt to understand him better. But I believe, and I am not alone in it, that he was once of the most lofty intelligences of his time. The *Revue de Paris* published two admirable letters of his in 1910, but there must be many more which it would be of the utmost importance to get to know. And his drawings – for Amiens, for Rouen, for Lyon, for Paris, for Marseilles, for Boston – they are so many acts of confidence, so marvellous, so full of substance. . . .

'Puvis de Chavannes was passionately concerned with art in its every manifestation. When Cézanne was first shown at Vollard's, Puvis was the most attentive of visitors. For he also aimed to renew the art of painting, and one could say that he succeeded. For instance he treated subjects, didn't he, that Chassériau had used before him? But he did them with an inspiration all his own! Like every other genius Puvis was ahead of his time. The experiments in stylization and in expressive synthesis which are typical of today's art were all present already in the art of Puvis.

'When he began he was at the mercy of the most contradictory tendencies. How did he know how to choose among so many temptations? That's what it would be invaluable to make clear today.

'Often his compositions began from an idea that was still imprecise – look at his first sketches! Then his intelligence went to work, and instead of losing the initial charm, as so often happens to others, he made it livelier still, and yet fresher. Puvis is a famous artist, but he is too much in the shadows. We need a proper book to bring him back to the light of mid-day. It would have a great deal to teach us.'

Germain Bazin

Vuillard Remembers Lautrec

An interview published in L'Amour de l'Art *(April 1931).*

It was in 1892 or 1893 that Vuillard met Lautrec. 'Bonnard and I had a little studio in the rue Pigalle. The *Revue Blanche* brought us all together – painters, critics, singers, writers – the whole Montmartre group.'

I asked if Degas was often in their company. 'No, Degas was very much a man on his own and very difficult to see. But Lautrec idolized him. When they first met, Degas looked at his canvases and said "Well, Monsieur, I can see that you're one of us." No tribute could have pleased him more. I remember how Lautrec gave a characteristic proof of his regard for Degas. It was in 1898 or 1899. Lautrec wanted to thank our friend Thadée Natanson for having us to stay at Villeneuve-sur-Yonne and he decided to give one of the gigantic dinners which were his speciality. He knew all the best dishes from all the best restaurants in Paris. Nothing was spared to give the luncheon a truly royal character. Lautrec had even brought some bottles of wine from his mother's cellar. At the end of the meal we were all in a highly excited state and we began to wonder what could possibly round off such a feast. Lautrec got up in the spur of the moment and led us off, without a word as to where we were going. We followed him with some apprehension all the way to the Dihaus' in the rue Frochot. Lautrec hauled himself up three flights of stairs to their apartment. Barely stopping to greet the Dihaus he led us up to Degas's painting *Dihau Playing in the Orchestra at the Opéra* and said "There you are – that's the dessert!" He could imagine no more wonderful treat to round off the meal than the sight of a Degas. So I can tell you that when I hear people disparage Degas by way of praising Lautrec I can imagine just how furious Lautrec would be.

'Degas and Lautrec rarely saw one another. Once or twice at the Dihaus',

The Widow's Visit   1899

IX   At the Opéra   *c.* 1900

perhaps. They didn't move in the same circles – 'the dance' meant the Opéra for Degas and the Moulin Rouge for Lautrec. And as you know Lautrec kept very odd company. . . .

'Yes, that prude Joyant said it was to be able to study the female nude quite freely and naturally instead of using professional models.

'It was much more complicated than that. Lautrec loathed hypocrisy, and quite possibly he did go, quite openly, in search of first-hand experience. But the real reasons for his behaviour were moral ones. . . . Lautrec was too proud to submit to his lot, as a physical freak, an aristocrat cut off from his kind by his grotesque appearance. He found an affinity between his own condition and the moral penury of the prostitute. He may have seemed cynical, but if he seemed so it was from an underlying despair. Though the most fastidious of men, he couldn't stay sober. Every night he was out with his boon companions – Maxime Dethomas and Romain Coolus were their chief representatives – going from bar to bar till at last they had to carry him home. I can only interpret his drunkenness as a deliberate act of suicide.

'I was always moved by the way in which Lautrec changed his tone when art was discussed. He who was so cynical and so foulmouthed on all other occasions became completely serious. It was a matter of faith with him.

'He dreaded being alone. His friendship was tyrannical and brooked no obstruction. Few men were more genuinely liked, by the way. Poor Lautrec! I went to see him one day in the rue Fronchot, just after he had been put in a home in Neuilly. He hadn't long to live. He was a dying man, a wreck. His doctor had told him to "take exercise", so he had bought a gymnasium-horse – he, Lautrec, who couldn't even get his feet on the pedals! A cruel irony – and yet it symbolized his whole life.'

Thadée Natanson

Vuillard as I Knew Him

At the end of his life, Thadée Natanson, in Peints à leur tour *(1948), put together a collection of articles, some substantial, some not, which related primarily to the circle of* La Revue Blanche. *Two of these were about Vuillard; what follows is an abridged version of one of them.*

It's true that Vuillard often used to stroke his nose from base to tip, but hardly enough, surely, to make it quite so sharp. I prefer to think that it sharpened itself, as one matures by experience. In his youth, perhaps that nose was not quite so pointed. But it must always have been sharp; it is so in the best portraits we have, painted by Bonnard, by Félix Vallotton, or by himself; in the delicate pencil sketch by Odilon Redon; and in Lacombe's bust. Yet formerly the first thing, and for a long time the chief thing, that struck one about Vuillard was the flaming red hair and beard that framed his face. This is inconceivable to those who only knew him when he was famous, or as the old man that he became, in appearance at any rate, very early; he was the first among his contemporaries whose hair-line receded into near-baldness and whose beard grew hoary. This appearance of age, however superficial, was misleading in the case of a man whose inquiring mind had lost none of its elasticity and whose ardour was that of an eighteen-year-old; not to mention his ceaselessly active sensitivity and his ever-fresh sensuous appetite.

What remained especially young in this attractive face was not only his smile, but above all those golden-brown eyes which only rarely darkened with anger and were usually glowing with kindness.

And yet those eyes, for ever busy provisioning his mind, were not easily accessible. Though never deliberately averted, they might be out harvesting, or modestly lowered. Vuillard ranks high among our French painters; and, though never taken in by worldly success, he cannot long have remained unaware of his own gifts. Yet he was always a person of the most genuine modesty. He was modest by nature, and his deeply religious upbringing had trained him, in childhood and then in youth, to humility. When he was very young this modesty seemed almost paradoxical in such a fiery-haired young man. Later, its gentle sweetness harmonized with the snowy whiteness that prematurely framed his face. From early youth, he had been convinced not so much of the vanity of all things as of their frailty, the frailty of man's mind as much as of his health, of happiness as of fine weather.

In his contacts with others, whoever they might be, he never sought to discover what they thought about him; his own feelings, of affection even more than of admiration, were all he needed to know. And this was equally true whether he was with Renoir or Monet, or with his own family; with Degas, or with Marc Mouclier or Auguste Bréal; with Mallarmé, Paul Valéry or Jean Giraudoux, or with some old acquaintance whose name was unknown to all but himself. True, moreover, with regard to the oldest or the newest of his women friends.

But I must also tell of his patience, which reflected the modesty of his heart.

This patience took many forms. First, a child's docility; later, that art of taking pains which every sort of talent needs in order, finally, to be recognized as genius. He was patient with the passions that carried him away; he was patient with his friends.

And never more patient than with his women friends.

And, in each case, his patience was greater than anyone else's.

We are all so full of ourselves that it is always a pleasant surprise to meet a man who thinks of other people. One is grateful for his interest in the being that each of us cherishes most, oneself, and one is even more eager to discuss that self with him. Of all the reasons for loving Vuillard the most delightful was that he convinced one of his love for oneself.

Disregard of self is one of the important rules of polite behaviour, and one of the surest ways of appearing lovable and, moreover, unconventional. Carried far enough, and when a person gives enough of himself, it makes up almost the whole of charity. With Vuillard it was never a pose, nor obedience to any principle; it was his natural way of being. It won him an enormous number of friends, but it was perfectly disinterested. So much disregard of self concealed, but did not stifle, an ardour which was equally basic to his nature. This ardour, although restrained, conferred an added glow to his modesty, since the effort made to conceal it only increased its strength.

In presence of another, all that concerned him personally seemed to him vain and indeed non-existent; he devoted himself entirely to that other. Many, if not most, people think only of what they can get out of whomever is speaking to them, whereas Vuillard thought only of how to help the other person. This abnegation ranged from an ever-ready obligingness to the unstinting gift of his whole being. Above all, the smile with which he would greet a casual acquaintance or a friend, or the dearest of his women friends, reflected a completely self-effacing modesty.

It was for reasons of the same nature that he so seldom exhibited his work, and that so few articles about it – not a single monograph, as far as I know – appeared in his lifetime. He discouraged journalists with great ingenuity, although without malice. And if he accepted nomination to the Institut, this was out of humility.

Vuillard's modesty was as invariable, as perfectly simple and unobtrusive, as the plain black clothes he wore or the loose bow tie that scarcely showed under his beard. He seemed like one of the black-clad figures in those Dutch paintings which delighted him so. Above the dark garments there gleamed those eyes which, one realized, discovered or disclosed the varied play of light, the enchanting colours of the visible world and the most elusive and tenuous fragment of those innumerable shades, of which the black that he wore represented not the absence, but the sum.

The unchanging severity of Vuillard's dress was the most striking of the differences between himself and Delacroix, for whom he had the warmest admiration. Delacroix, on the contrary, liked to wear something vivid and took trouble over his appearance. Otherwise they had more than one trait in common. Both were in love with colour, both sensitive to music. Vuillard was the more scrupulously loyal to his friends for their own sake. I don't know which of them was more avid for intimate friendship with women – not, however, with one at a time – or which of them repaid with greater tenderness, and an attachment that came close to bondage, the care and affection with which he delighted to be surrounded. But if certain notebooks have been found in which Vuillard sometimes set down his private thoughts, these by no means constitute a journal such as Delacroix kept for most of his life; and no publisher ever persuaded Vuillard to write the least scrap of an article on any of the painters he loved best, whether Poussin or Bonnard. And yet in every letter, in every note he ever wrote, we catch a gleam of that way of looking at things and people, and of reflecting on them, which is as completely individual as the exquisite tracery of his handwriting.

Historically and logically, sensibility precedes intelligence. In Vuillard's mind they grew up side by side.

He was born in 1868 at Cuiseaux in the Jura, a little town nearer to Lons-le-Saunier than to Dôle, Pasteur's birthplace, close to the Arbois vine-growing region and not very far from Courbet's Ornans. His father, a retired officer, had been appointed tax-collector there. He was a sensitive and particularly affectionate child, who was made much of by everybody, not only by his own family; at home, he was cherished by an elderly father and a brother and sister much older than himself, but above all by his mother, who found her greatest happiness in making him happy. He was a good child rather than a quiet one. The ardent feelings which already he could scarcely master were only partly satisfied by the little world in which he lived and of which his mother, a well-loved Parisienne, was the radiant centre. Nor did he succeed in devoting the rest of his fervour to God, for his piety only intensified the fire that human affection had fostered.

When his parents took him back to Paris with them, he never forgot Cuiseaux. Later on, even till he was an old man, he was often to return to visit the friends whose loyal remembrance touched him and the places where he had spent his happy childhood and his mother most of her life. At fifteen, his religious faith was strong enough to enable him to stop in the middle of the rue Auber and, in order to mortify human vanity, slowly and publicly to make the sign of the cross.

Of that piety nothing was to remain, once he had lost his faith on growing up; but certain tender memories that persisted, and that ardour – I should like to call it naked – which was to inspire him until his dying day.

The tender intimacy of home life, those religious feelings and the ardour that outlived them, were the springs that fed Vuillard's sensibility as a young man. These were the warm springs; there were others, the chilliest of which was *ennui*. The pale, shy, red-haired youth, deprived of almost everything, introverted, undecided, anxious about the future and tormented by his own ardent nature, felt himself a burden even more to himself than to his family, and gave way to depression. All his mother's vitality and wisdom were powerless to save him. And yet as his intelligence grew stronger, he succeeded in controlling depression by means of thought. Henceforward, as he came to understand his sufferings, his sensibility drew sustenance from them: from the aridity of boredom, from anxiety about the future, from the nightmare of scruples and mental paralysis – not from doubt, which is virile, but from self-doubt. These psychological troubles are not exclusively childish ailments. But from these, and from subsequent relapses, Vuillard's intelligence always found ingenious ways of rescuing his sensibility.

As a lad, he would become absorbed in contemplation of the windows opening on to the street, or the repetitive pattern of wallpaper. Living a lonely life in the apartment where his widowed mother had courageously set up a sewing workroom – the sight of the girls at work was invaluable to him as a painter – equally isolated at home or out of doors, and most of all in a crowd, occupied less with reading than with daydreaming, he grew ever more acutely and painfully sensitive. From this state of *ennui*, which was later to recur from time to time, his intelligence drew forth reflections which were to be of lasting benefit. Even before they had borne fruit, we can recognize their gloomy, highly personal blossoms in the painter's first apprentice efforts. And the sap that was to fill the fruit rose from the same roots.

Meanwhile, however, nothing quite took his mind off himself – neither the Académie Julian, nor the newspaper offices and theatres that he frequented, nor the youthful friends he had begun to make, nor any of the other activities which he came to enjoy, and which fostered his talent. Nothing could restrain that ardent soul of his, until its tumult at last subsided, leaving him inevitably as distressed as before. Nothing could save it but the affection of his mother and of a few friends such as Pierre Hermant and Paul Percheron, and the passionate and undying friendship he formed with K.-X. Roussel, who was to become his brother-in-law. His relations with others, such as his friendship with Maurice Denis and Lautrec and the far closer bond with Bonnard, came later. As for his friendships with women, they only added to his perturbation of spirit.

The youth who had found life so tedious became one of the most sensitive painters of our time, indeed perhaps of all time. And he was one of the most sensuous, in an art that is based almost wholly on sensuousness. His sensitivity and his sensuousness led him to overstrain his faculties and to experience joys as acute as pains. His intelligence purified these, and taught him to express them with ever more delicate nuances, whose natural subtlety was always controlled by reason. At first some of his inventions may have seemed obscure; in certain lithographs and paintings he reveals the unexpected simply by expressing his personality. But each time, his ever keener and more questing sensuousness was governed by intelligence. He was receptive to impressions, constantly, unremittingly, almost tirelessly. Thus there arose a state of intense emotion, a kind of love, for things as well as for human beings, which was to possess him ever after. Wherever he was, his sensitivity and his intelligence were at work, fastening on everything, constantly and feverishly.

Among familiar objects, before a jug in which anemones were unfolding, or in the country, in ecstasy before a convolvulus or the vanishing lines of a hill, this twofold activity was as unceasing as a bee's. Or again, at home, when gazing at a Degas or a Corot, or at his own interpretation of Cézanne's face, or at photographs of paintings by Watteau or Vermeer or outsize reproductions of Michelangelo, and even more when watching his mother, for ever by his side – her tiny person, her busy movements, her lively glances. The intensity of his attention to this beloved model, who inspired him so constantly and so happily, accounts for the masterpieces which the painter in him wrested from the son's devotion. But all his mental powers were equally alert, as ready to take advantage of a Maillol or a Tanagra statuette as of the eyes and gestures of the friends who visited him. And amid all these, majestic without arrogance, a full-size cast of the Venus of Milo had dwelt, for as long as anyone could remember, in the home of the painter and his family. This Venus brought her own magnificence into the jumble of furniture, household objects, half-finished works and other paraphernalia that filled the room that was more particularly Vuillard's studio.

When he greeted his visitors with a smile, and even more when he was busy painting, among the little pots where his colours, mixed with glue, were simmering on the stove, his smock stiff with splashes of paint, there were many moments of such vibrant emotion that one felt that not only Vuillard's heart but his whole mind were laid bare. He lived between the friends whom he watched talking, who would shortly leave him, and the dearly loved mother who stayed, but who would not always stay with him, and the great block of plaster with its coating of dust, more familiar and more living than any marble, that other splendid, impressive companion of his every hour, which would outlive them all.

To stir his senses and increase his mental activity he needed only the windows of his flat, opening – as in the rue de la Tour, of old – on to a market gardener's plot, or, later, in the Place Vintimille with its playing children and its birds, its greenery and its crowded benches. Or the walks of any other garden, large or small, for he was happy in them all; less, however, in the Champs-Elysées than in the Tuileries, through whose time-honoured Parisian scenes, past whose statues and fountains, he often passed on his way to the Louvre. And it took no more than the lighting of a lamp in a friend's house, or a woman's blouse as she bent forward, or simply a cushion or the corner of a carpet, to set his mind working. The wild tumult within him resulted for our benefit in a world of enchantment. Sometimes, indeed, it took no more than the idle table-talk, tossed to and fro above the glasses, of which he often caught no more than the mere noise. It was in private conversation, when alone he could feel really himself, that his whole being was most fully extended.

And again, in the countryside near Cuiseaux, or in the Yonne, or around Paris, which he loved and studied so attentively – indeed in every place, from every morning till every evening, under all kinds of light, Vuillard lived with all the strength of his soul, among the shapes of things, never separating lines from colour, never dividing 'the cluster that the Gods kept so closely knit': *la touffe . . . Que les Dieux gardaient si bien mêlée* (Mallarmé, 'L'Après-midi d'un faune').

Avidly, he fed his sensitivity upon these forms, but still required his intelligence to devise ever new methods of imposing order on them.

This work, his hard but beloved task, this twofold activity, took up every instant of all his instants. He felt that he was being flayed alive, but he revelled in it. If he did not speak, it was because he had not time. Barely time to eat. Or to smile.

Vuillard's heart was no less sensitive than his mind, and no less continuously sensitive. The fierce ardour of his heart equalled the subtlety of his mind. The heart's sensitivity has a feminine kind of delicacy. Vuillard had, moreover, an active gift of intuition. He would listen to confidences solely in order to relieve the man who was confiding in him or the woman who was in distress; but he suffered from their tears long before the first was shed. Even the selfishness of happiness moved him, and his heart responded to misfortune as his mind did to the innumerable effects of light. Of the only two classes he distinguished, he was always on the side of the poor, even though he had learnt the painful secrets of many of his wealthy friends. He was often deceived; I don't think he ever regretted it. If he found that he had given help in a case of bogus misfortune, he would rejoice at there being one real misfortune the less. But the world would have seemed to him more bearable if there had been only material misfortunes to relieve. He never failed to give his help, to either sort; as much as possible, and more and more.

When he brought himself to talk – which he would only do in private – his conversation revealed that the riches harvested by his sensitivity had not only benefited his paintings. His subtlest and tenderest qualities were lavished on a few chosen friends. And he constantly strove to know these better, not with any wish to judge them but purely to learn a little more so as to have more to cherish. He took pleasure in sharing the bounty of himself among all his friends, and yet, with that rare capacity of very loving hearts, he would give the whole of himself to each of them, so intensely that no friend could feel jealous. In the case of his woman friends, it was another matter. And yet he would never rob one in order to satisfy another's demand for affection, even if she sought more than her share – since women are tyrannical not only for the pleasure of it, but through that greed implied by the Latin word for the sin of avarice [*gola*]. And in the evening, at least every evening of those best years when he still had his mother with him, Vuillard was able to enjoy being unreservedly hers. They did not need many words to talk about this or that, for they were at one in their feelings, each one's sensitivity being born of the other.

In the son's case, despite the subtle refinement which his sensitivity acquired, his intelligence enabled it to skirt the near-abnormal unscathed. And that intelligence, having taught the painter to turn to account the most delicate and elusive of his emotions, was equally able to discipline every reverberation of that sensitivity, even at its most vulnerable, in his heart as well as in his mind. These faculties interacted in mutual support, as though his sensitivity were affected by increasingly ineffable sensations while his intelligence worked out ever more refined means of expressing them. Not to mention that one of the strongest roots of sensitivity – in Vuillard's case as in that of Rousseau – is sensuousness.

And yet by dint of tension the springs of this over-delicate and over-active mechanism sometimes snapped. There were moments when this extremely reserved man would drop all affability, and, seeming utterly transformed, would yield to that passion which he had lost the power to restrain.

Some kind friends had arranged a reconciliation between Vuillard and a lady with whom he had had a quarrel, the complicated causes of which not even Proust could have unravelled; the whole ceremony had been planned, down to the sequence of words to be exchanged. But when he reached the garden seat where the injured lady was waiting, what Vuillard actually vociferated was one single word, three times repeated – the ultimate oath.

Many years previously, at the time of the Dreyfus affair, on the evening when the news of the Rennes verdict reached the house where Vuillard was spending the summer, his eyes brimmed fuller of tears than those of any of his companions, who were about to join him in commiseration for the condemned man. They heard an unrecognizable voice declare: 'I don't give a damn about Dreyfus. It's my country I weep for.' And, brushing everyone aside, he went to shut himself up in his room.

The sweetness of his smile wiped out the memory of such brief storms an hour after. Others were repressed, and lasted longer. During the two world wars his sensitivity was often stirred to compassion or exasperation, and his baffled intelligence caused him equal distress. In the first war, during which he served as a track-watchman for several months, he suffered less: the Germans' methodical ferocity had not yet found its full scope. But from the beginning of the prolonged prelude to the second (the end of which he did not live to see), he was too close a witness to the intrigues of the political parties and of some of their leaders. The silence which he enforced upon himself was a source of much suffering to him.

The wonders discovered by those world-travellers whose tales excite us most are always inherent in themselves. Others had met the same faces, had seen the same monuments in the same places; if none of them caught the wonder or saw the light, it was because they had not been blessed with the gift of insight. Vuillard never exercised his insight far afield, being a stay-at-home by nature; he spent his life between his own home, which for a long time meant his mother's, and those of a very few friends. A narrow space, in which he none the less discovered more than is in all the Vuillards in existence, even including those which exist only as drafts or sketches. And yet that is enough to change his admirers' way of looking at the world, almost their whole lives. For he achieves no less than such a transformation.

It was to his gift of insight, moreover, that he owed his profound understanding of the books he read. From the catechism and the Bible stories of his childhood up to Sainte-Beuve's *Volupté*, the first book perhaps in which, as a passionate youth, he drank his fill of heart-searchings, and found stimulation for his sensual nature; or again up to Taine's *Intelligence*, on many of whose theories he reflected deeply, particularly the theory of signs. But I believe that no writer except, later, Mallarmé, enriched his newly developing mind so much as Buffon. These were some of the authors who were most important to him, at least in the early days. He went on reading all his life, though never for the sake of having read a book, or of talking about it, but always from an urge to learn. He read in all sincerity, just as he always had to hand the basic information to be got from dictionaries. It was thus that among other things he read everything extant by Delacroix and Baudelaire, a great many books not only about painters and the fine arts but about every kind of subject, even politics (starting with Cardinal de Retz), and including, page by page, the nine thick volumes of Henri Brémond's *Histoire du sentiment religieux en France*. This did not prevent him from reading freely among contemporary writers, and not only his friends such as Paul Valéry or Jean Giraudoux. He studied Mallarmé with particular care, and went so far as to discover beneath the images and cadences of 'L'Après-midi d'un faune' a whole Art of Poetry.

To talk with Vuillard about a book that he had read often brought one the joy of getting to know the author whom he had discovered. He never read a book in order to recognize himself in it; rather, like those who have suffered from much depression, he read to be taken completely out of himself. Far from 'reading between the lines', he lingered over each line, extracting all that he could from it.

Women are so much accustomed to being treated with indulgence that they scarcely yearn for it; but for them it is a keener pleasure to find someone who understands them – and since they find it hard to read their own hearts clearly, and feel the burden of the whole world upon them, nothing seems to them more uncommon. He had to understand them in order to teach them so much about themselves, and yet remain obedient.

Vuillard may at times have fallen for women whom everyone admired; he may even have figured among the thousand and three victims of some female Don Giovanni. But others attracted him more durably: those who were unregarded, unseen. Was it by chance, or from sheer modesty? Did he take particular delight in those that others neglected? Or was it perhaps that, in his relations with the unfortunate, he had more of himself to contribute? It mattered so little that for others they lacked attraction! In the same way the things that he loved as a painter were not those generally considered charming or remarkable; his gifts alone made them delectable.

To such women, once despised and now, to their own amazement, proud, he offered more than the ephemeral pleasure of surprise. The humblest of them could now taste the joy of ruling over a mind as rich as his. His admiration, the admiration of a famous painter, seemed to each one to prove the reality of her charm – of which she, if no one else, had always been convinced.

There were women in plenty to take advantage of Vuillard's readiness to be confided in. It was a habit his mother had taught him. They could be friends or confidants, models (those of his portraits rather than of his studies), visitors, art collectors, or the merely curious; ladies anxious to enrich their salons; girls barely out of childhood, or faded belles: Vuillard, the bachelor, was never without feminine company. He could have been entirely satisfied with what, for La Fontaine, was only 'one half of this world's blessings'. Each of his women friends was precious to him. Sensuousness is close to emotional sensitivity, and nobody who has ever seen a Vuillard painting can doubt the keenness of his senses. These were heart-to-heart dialogues, in which he gave freely of himself, even to the point of exhaustion. Many displays of affection that delighted him might well have been dictated by self-interest; but one could scarcely venture to resent this unless one was oneself completely disinterested. And he was well aware that disinterestedness is not a feminine virtue, except where it accompanies passion. He needed only the delicate contact of his women friends, the fragrance – whether natural or not – of their desire to please. He was able to use his insight in dealing with the simplest creatures, just as one needs it with animals and, when one loves them, with plants. In souls of such fine quality, it is a gift never withheld. The insight with which Vuillard

Child in a Room *c.* 1900

XI The Painter Ker-Xavier Roussel and his Daughter *c.* 1904

XII   The Café Wepler   *c.* 1905

XIII   Marthe Mellot: the Garden Gate   1910

XIV   Annette on the Beach at Villerville   1910–11

treated all his women friends sprang from his intelligence as much as from his sensitivity. And his sensuous instincts often contributed to it.

The last time I saw Vuillard was at the beginning of June 1940. He was already threatened by the disease that was eventually to lay him low. Our unhappiness, which united us more closely than ever, was not made up only of disappointments. We dared not even say how much we were alarmed by the defeat of all that represented humanity for us, nor how great were our fears.

We began talking about the correspondence between Renan and Berthelot after 1871, which I had just been rereading. They were both astonished and disturbed by the *débâcle* and its consequences, and equally preoccupied by memories of the Commune, which had impressed them powerfully. Then we talked about the two men's characters; the reason and energy which had always sustained Berthelot and the tender humanity of Renan. Vuillard hesitated as he sought to define the quality of Renan's love for Jesus. Meanwhile he was playing with a china saucer which he had picked up from a small table. Held thus between his fingers, it seemed to have no thickness, only colour – even less than that, because of its transparency.

Annette Vaillant

Monsieur Vuillard

Madame Annette Vaillant is the daughter of Alfred Natanson, co-founder of La Revue Blanche, *and of Marthe Mellot, the gifted actress who appears in many of Vuillard's paintings. The two texts reprinted here date from the 1960s and first appeared as catalogue-prefaces for, respectively, the Galerie Durand-Ruel ('Vuillard', 1961) and the Galerie Maeght ('Autour de la Revue Blanche', 1966).*

Being a pampered child, freely admitted to the company of my elders, I used from an early age to be on first-name terms with most of my father's friends. But there was one whom affection mingled with respect led me to treat differently. Using, for him alone, the English form of polite address, I called him reverently and for ever: 'Monsieur Vuillard'.

Through wartime and peacetime, schooldays and holidays, as far back as I can remember, he was there: from the time I first learnt to walk at L'Etang-la-Ville, with Annette and Jacques Roussel, his niece and nephew, until that May morning in 1940 when we parted in the avenue du Bois. He was finishing the portrait of Madame Wertheimer, who lived in the same house as General Gamelin. Reassuring rumours ran through our offices: the army was standing firm, no need to worry. Yet a strange, intense stillness hung over the splendour of the chestnut trees. Jos Hessel, taciturn as ever, had brought us back from our last weekend at Les Clayes. I held out my hand, then my cheek, as usual: 'Au revoir, Monsieur Vuillard.' How could I have guessed that it was 'goodbye', that he was at the close of his life, that we were all nearing the end of something that had been so easy for so long, and that a few weeks later, as the exodus scattered us, I should learn through a couple of frigid lines that his fragile heart, rejecting the catastrophe, had ceased to beat, that despair had killed him?

Never again were we to spend happy summer days with him at Les Clayes. Nothing is left today of the burnt-down house but two dead turrets; but there still remain, more living than any relic, the pictures he painted in his ground-floor room: a pot of pink geraniums before a mirror that reflects the trees of the Ile-de-France; his studio-bedroom with its narrow bed and all his battery of pots of glue.

In her casual morning dress, Madame Hessel – his lifelong friend, whose youthful jet-black hair had become the white halo of the portrait he painted in the rue de Naples – Lucie Hessel, her secateurs in her gloved hand, arranged huge bouquets. Leaning forward, his eyes ready to pounce, he would in a flash set down in his sketch-book the exact look of her as she held the branches. How many sketches I have seen him make! Peering gimlet-eyed over his spectacles, he often pinned down our attitudes at play or caught us unawares, with cup raised, at breakfast in the garden.

Looking backwards over his work, I retrace the stages of my life from 1940 to my early childhood. From the glades of Vaucresson to Cabourg (where Vuillard was then painting Madame Gosset's portrait – I can still see the daffodil-yellow cushion). From the boulevard Malesherbes to Loctudy, where with Annette and Jacques Roussel I raced along the windswept Breton shore. Last summer, revisiting Loctudy as one revisits a graveyard, I found the house overshadowed by tall trees and the verandah grown dark, whereas its summer-morning brightness lives for-ever in his great luminous panels. In the same way, not long ago, I suddenly met my mother on the wall of a picture gallery; there she sat, embroidering, in her yellow peignoir, with a white shawl over her shoulders.

In Paris Madame Vuillard, a little, round, home-loving person, would sit reading the paper by the window, her feet on a foot-warmer, the serene image of self-sacrifice rewarded. Or else she might be playing a polka at full speed on her un-pretentious upright piano. We interrupted her with a ring at the bell when we called, at the rue de Calais, my father holding me by the hand. Monsieur Vuillard, an exquisitely considerate son, was happy to be with the mother he worshipped in her well-polished paradise, and yet – a lively magician in his schoolteacher's garb – he was equally at home painting Elisabeth Bibesco in her house at the tip of the Ile Saint-Louis, or in the rue Scheffer sitting by Anna de Noailles's bed, to which silk fringes tangled with the telephone wires gave an Oriental air.

Women loved him as he loved them, whether they were princesses, actresses or stay-makers. But while he took pleasure in the cunning effects of shaded lights in over-rich drawing-rooms, he preferred the familiar rites of home, the decent red-edged tablecloth folded after the evening meal.

White tablecloths, checked tablecloths of our Normandy tea-parties at Viller-ville; I recognize the lady visitors in their great hats, and the armchairs of plaited straw, bought from gipsies for one summer season's use by the seaside.

What happened to the fantastic silk stockings – violet, absinthe-green, tango, lemon-coloured – that Mother kept in a casket? He had given them to her for Christmas. Gone, too, is my charming Japanese tea-set on its pretty bamboo tray; Monsieur Vuillard's presents were like no one else's. Nor were his outbursts of anger: for this model of kindness and tolerance, always intensely sensitive, flared up at times. Should one, with thoughtless irony, decry something about which, in secret, he felt deeply; should one dare to suggest that Puvis de Chavannes . . . he would fly into a passion. Losing all self-control, he would utter terrible words. I think the saints must be like that, too.

Here we are, then, my sister and I, spade in hand, a dog at our feet, small creatures from that world of his that belongs to another age, when fine summers seemed eternal. Thanks to him, many years from now, if Heaven preserves this painting which I love, the little girl that I have long ceased to be will go on living. She wears a woollen bodice under her thin taffeta frock. Her tiny hands clutch the hard wooden arms of her chair. My father sits on the old-fashioned sofa, whose long cushion gleams with unfaded brightness; he is reading aloud *Le Compagnon de voyage*, a story which I scarcely understand but which I feel is sad. Shall I, too, travel alone some day along the road? Or will the door that leads into the past swing open, and will my mother come in, young and gay? And then Monsieur Vuillard – with his round-toed boots, his soft collar, his slender bow-tie, the clean smell of his honey-coloured beard – will bend over to kiss me before, once again, he starts to clean his paintbrushes.

Annette Vaillant

La Revue Blanche

Words overheard but not understood: a child's imagination associated them with an image that survives as an intact mirage from the remote, remembered past. I was four years old.

In our house, as the grown-ups talked, I seemed to see a shroud spread over that snow-clad princess, lying in a swoon, whose name recurred so often: *La Revue Blanche*.

Whispered more secretly in the servants' quarters – with what unanimously admiring and yet shocked regret – soft as a caress, sharp as a scratch, I caught the name of Misia, 'Madame Thadée', my uncle's wife; their divorce must have followed close on the disappearance of *La Revue Blanche*. Were these two the same young woman, extravagant and too dearly loved?

On Toulouse-Lautrec's poster, Misia comes towards you with her fur necklet, her lovely little frozen face tense under her spotted veil. She personifies *La Revue Blanche*, which I confused with this elegant, self-confident creature, daringly yet meticulously dressed, symbol of that *fin-de-siècle* intelligentsia which intermarried with the upper bourgeoisie.

It was at Spa in 1889 that, from the excited discussions of some very young men on holiday – Joe Hogge, Auguste Jeunhomme de Paix, the two Leclercq brothers and my father (still a schoolboy: the youngest of the Natansons) – from these young minds, intoxicated with literature, thirsty for unfamiliar fruits and eager for self-expression, the idea of *La Revue Blanche* was born.

When they returned to Paris, the fever spread through the classrooms of the Lycée Condorcet. Short-lived poems and shrewd criticism proliferated and soon began to display their artless boldness in the slender issues of the very first *Revue Blanche*. Published at Liège, it lasted two years; this Belgian series is practically unobtainable today.

The Parisian series (it was to survive twelve years, from 1891 to 1903) was edited by my father's elder brothers, Alexandre and, more particularly, Thadée.

The magazine was run, to begin with, from a private house in the avenue des Champs-Elysées, the home of Paul Leclercq's parents. Later, as a charming bachelor and an unassuming poet, author of *Ibis*, irrevocably in love with Polaire, Paul Leclercq was to scatter rose-petals all up the staircase for the visits of that wasp-waisted siren.

Before long the Parisian *Revue Blanche* – that 'rallying-centre for the most divergent tendencies', according to Gide – held its first editorial meetings at the back of a courtyard in the rue des Martyrs. Then followed the long period in the rue Lafitte and the boulevard des Italiens.

'The friendly *Revue Blanche*, open to all comers', as Mallarmé was to say, welcomed every sort of talent, all new ideas, at the period when Barrès was still God for Lucien Mühlfeld and for Léon Blum, then a twenty-year-old student at the Ecole Normale with a flower in his buttonhole. Mühlfeld and Blum acted in turn as literary critic to the *Revue*, preceding Gide whose first contributions were 'Paludes', 'Saül' and 'Philoctète'.

A universal eclecticism found room, between the neo-Christian gospel of Tolstoy and the refined anarchism of Fénéon, that subtle mandarin of the 'Procès des Trente', for the misty gloom of Scandinavian dramas. Thus my favourite cousin Bolette got her first name from Ibsen: Ibsen, the pompous, surly old man of genius, whom Munch portrayed on a theatre programme with all his self-satisfied severity and his artfully dishevelled tufts of white hair.

Robert Dreyfus and Marcel Proust made their appearance here; former pupils of the Lycée Condorcet, like Fernand Gregh, and survivors from the wreck of the short-lived *Banquet*. Proust was later to include in *Les Plaisirs et les jours* certain 'Etudes' which were first published in *La Revue Blanche*. From further afield, Apollinaire contributed 'L'Hérésiarque'. And when a little girl in a red dress, the eldest daughter of my elder uncle, was brought along to the rue Lafitte 'to say hullo', Verlaine, at the close of his unsteady life, sat down at the corner of a table and wrote a sonnet for her.

The official reception day at the *Revue* was Thursday, but friends dropped in every day; and at the time of the Dreyfus affair, although everyone was in agreement, passionate discussions were carried on until the small hours.

The list of contributors to *La Revue Blanche* included Verlaine and Mallarmé, Claudel, Wilde, Péguy, Jean Lorrain and Viélé-Griffin, Regnier and Rémy de Gourmont, Zola, Moréas and Jarry. Francis Jammes, uttering beautiful girls' names in a Béarnais accent like a belch of garlic. Charles-Louis Philippe, the poet of penury, offering a glimpse into sordid attic dwellings. And Dr Mardrus, husband of 'Princess Amanda', the imitator of animal noises. Mardrus's translation of the *Arabian Nights*, published in serial form and carefully kept from the curious young, sent André Gide into raptures.

There was Julien Benda, assiduously crabbed, and Mirbeau with his frenzied kindness, and Jules (*Poil de Carotte*) Renard, who signed his tart 'Tablettes d'Eloi' with a tiny fox from Lautrec's *Histoires naturelles*; and Claude Terrasse, and Franc-Nohain, that delightful precursor of Jacques Prévert, and Alphonse Allais, and Tristan Bernard, who gave a note of inimitable humour to the magazine. Debussy, brought along by his friend Pierre Louÿs, had already become 'Monsieur Croche' in order to demolish Massenet.

The list may seem too long, but it is by no means complete. What can I say about those who played a leading part and whose names no longer reflect the importance they had at the time: men like Barrucand and Fagus, Gustave Kahn, or the tumultuously prolific Paul Adam?

At Etretat, that fashionable seaside resort favoured by the youthful intelligentsia, the three daughters of Narcisse Meyer had their train of admirers. The eldest married Paul Adam. The second, who had a lovely face, suffered from a malformation of the lower limbs which won her the nickname of *la belle Otarie*, the fair sea-lion. This mermaid was to marry Lucien Mühlfeld, soon to become a bemonocled dandy; after his death she devoted herself to her literary salon on the right bank. Meanwhile the youngest of the three sisters, a fascinating creature, had become Madame Cappiello, at the time when the hoardings of Paris displayed Cappiello's poster for Thermogène wool, with its leaping flames.

Cappiello had contributed to a special number of *La Revue Blanche* a delightfully mischievous set of caricatures of the most popular Parisian actresses of the day, from Sarah Bernhardt to Réjane and from Jeanne Granier to Lavallière.

Meanwhile Lautrec, whose posters of Bruant in a red neckcloth and Jane Avril with her foaming petticoats made cabbies turn round and stare, would turn up at the rue Lafitte escorted by Tapié de Celeyran, his favourite stooge.

Perched on one of the huge green leather settees in the vestibule, king and jester to a worshipping coterie was that fascinating monster Lautrec. When not commenting on Balzac even more brilliantly than Proust would do, he was grinding his words like pebbles, sniffling and laughing until the tears came into his eyes, those excessively beautiful eyes, magnified by his glasses. Every wish of his was promptly complied with: the setting-up of his *NIB* for a joke, or the preparation of a lithographic stone with the single imprint of two scarlet lips.

Tristan Bernard, who was director of the Vélodrome Buffalo, shared with Lautrec a passion for cycle races. Léon Blum and Fénéon, unusual sports reporters, had co-opted as a third member of their team Romain Coolus, that many-sided and faithful contributor to *La Revue Blanche* from its first number to its last.

Who remembers Romain Coolus, with his poems in the manner of Banville, his boulevard comedies, and his puns? He was short and sturdy, with a crooked face, a scholar with a hoarse voice and a cracked laugh; Lautrec bullied him like an affectionate tyrant, forcing him to stay for weeks on end in the rue d'Amboise or the rue des Moulins, sharing the company of Rolande or Carmen or Mireille and the leg of mutton carved by Monsieur.

'Colette!' (it was his teasing nickname for Coolus), 'Colette! Sit there, I'm going to do your portrait.'

In his portrait in the Albi museum, Coolus no longer looks like the young philosophy teacher, mad about Mallarmé, that he once was. Much later, as an old bachelor drinking cocoa-and-water in the garden, one summer holiday, he managed to get into my stubborn head one of the *Chansons bas* that he had published in 1892 in *La Revue Blanche*: and the fragrance of *ta paille azure de lavandes* ('your lavender-blue straw') scents my childhood for ever.

Valvins meant Mallarmé: his meticulously ordered table, the regal poverty of his room, his gleaming little boat with its white sails.

His summer neighbours, Thadée Natanson and his bride, had just settled in at La Grangette. In the attic, the light shone through a green opaline lampshade on to the little pictures that Vuillard painted during the quiet evenings.

On fine days La Grangette became an informal branch of *La Revue Blanche*. But in late autumn, after 'his ladies' had gone back to Paris, Mallarmé would come round in the evenings for dinner, wearing his long overcoat and carrying his lamp. Perfectly turned out, in his worn jacket and the spotless little black slippers he kept on when he took off his sabots, he would sit for hours listening to Misia at the piano.

Aile que du papier déploie
Bats toute si t'initia
Naguère à l'orage et la joie
De son piano Misia

'Paper wing unfolding, flutter fully if Misia once initiated you into the storm and joy of her piano', he wrote on a fan for her.

Lautrec, too, adored listening to Misia when she played Beethoven and Schubert. But Mallarmé did not like Lautrec's coarse jokes; he hated the language of Jarry's *Ubu*. Mirbeau, stylishly dressed like a well-to-do country gentleman, sometimes brought along Jarry, who always wore a cyclist's outfit and boots laced with velvet ribbons.

How could these mocking imps, these rowdy boozers, fail to offend Mallarmé, who with such exquisite manners offered the dazzled visitors to his bare rooms in the rue de Rome a glass of sugared water?

Misia, Fauré's beloved pupil, gay and whimsical, with her winning ways and her bluntness and the swagger of a low-life princess, was none the less everyone's muse. She was to reign more unconstrainedly in the following years at Le Relais, a big eighteenth-century house that had been a coaching inn, an enchanting place always full of friends and laughter. It was here that a few summers later I took my first steps, between Aunt Misia and my mother.

Marthe Mellot was a young actress – in a Symbolist tunic, she had played Antonia, Edouard Dujardin's heroine – who had come to know *La Revue Blanche* through its painters. They had designed her costumes, and in the workshops of the Bouffes du Nord they had painted the scenery for the Théâtre de l'Œuvre.

For a second-rate play by Jean Richepin, performed at the Théâtre Antoine – *La Gitane* – in which Marthe Mellot played the lead, Lautrec was to provide, in 1900, his last poster, like the vivid flare-up of a dying brand. The following year Alfred Natanson (others might speak better than I can of his modesty, his sensitive charm and the affection he inspired) and Marthe Mellot, my future father and mother, were married.

Bonnard, Vuillard and Roussel were lifelong friends of our family; they became deeply devoted to my father, and were fascinated by Thadée, that gorgeous silk-shirted Assyrian colossus, who unfortunately could not resist the lure of the precarious enterprises that ran him into debt, to the whole family's detriment.

Bonnard, Vuillard and Roussel: I could not, and I still cannot, dissociate their names. Long before my birth they had played bowls with Coolus and Vallotton on the gravel walks of Villeneuve, while Lautrec, shouting 'Tally-ho! Tally-ho!' chased bees with his little walking-stick.

In several of the pictures painted by Vuillard at Le Relais during this period I recognize the rustic seats, woven in the Albi region, which Lautrec sent to his friends.

With his secret sarcasm and his pale, disturbing eyes, cutting as the north wind, Félix Vallotton distilled with cruel skill and ice-cold intelligence the poison of his painful experiences. As for Maurice Denis, the theorist with an angelic gaze, every-thing he painted – a child's cheek or an apple – gave out a kind of radiance.

Of their kind older friend, Odilon Redon, Denis would say that he was the Mallarmé of painting.

Thadée loved these 'thinking painters' whose work in black and white or in colour he published in his magazine. They often foregathered in the rue Lafitte – while Fénéon went on unconcernedly correcting proofs – and with them was their good friend Sérusier, that cheerful prophet, subtle dialectician, complicated teacher and hearty drinker. And Paul Ranson, too early dead, that bizarre aesthete who designed stylized feminine shapes intertwined, like arabesques, with tangled branches: he found relaxation in outrageous clowning. Before *Ubu*, Ranson had created for his puppet theatre the unprecedented character of the Abbé Prout.

Charles Cottet also died young; he was a stout, red-bearded, jovial Savoyard who had been one of the first to discover Brittany – a very different Brittany from Gauguin's.

Ibels loved the circus, acrobatics on horseback, the entry of the clowns, and the lively colours of the *comique troupier* [barrack-room farce].

Hermann-Paul put a ferocious irony into the drawings he courageously pub-lished at the time of the Dreyfus affair. Much later, I learned to appreciate his clear elegance.

Rippl Ronaï, a friend of Maillol's, arrived in Paris with a thick moustache and the folk-songs of his native Hungary; he always breakfasted off bacon soaked in paprika. He was later to return to Budapest to rebuild the homes of Magyar princes in Art Nouveau style.

The day after Mallarmé's funeral, when his friends had followed his coffin to the little graveyard of Samoreau on a fine September afternoon, they all assembled at Le Relais. Renoir sat beside Misia on a bench in front of the house, his narrow face drawn and wrinkled, his shaggy hair already grey. Bonnard was there, seen from the back; Renoir had written to him: 'You have a touch of enchantment. . . . It's a precious gift.' Bonnard's drawings for *Marie*, that exquisite book published by *La Revue Blanche*, had delighted him. The flower-like figure of Marie was inspired by Marthe, who was already, and was to remain, the uneasy, tormenting sprite in Bonnard's life.

But the bending figures, like toiling graces, that merge into the patterned wall-paper, were devoutly studied by Vuillard in the evenings at his mother's modest home. And Vuillard painted the forest where I wandered as a little girl, with its endless rippling green: a landscape more real than reality, on the wall at my grand-father's. And those landscapes round L'Etang-la-Ville which for Roussel were Arcadia.

Bonnard, Vuillard, Roussel. Friends' faces. No need to hunt far in one's memory. I have only to close my eyes to see them, and remember.

Jacques Salomon

Vuillard Remembered

During the last twenty years of Vuillard's life he saw a great deal of his nephew by marriage, Jacques Salomon. Himself primarily a painter, M. Salomon was well equipped to profit by the unique opportunities which presented themselves; and after Vuillard's death he set himself to record what he remembered of Vuillard, both as a painter and as a man. There followed a series of books in which M. Salomon has given lively and delicate expression to his memories of Vuillard. The first group of extracts given here is from Auprès de Vuillard *(Paris 1953); 'Vuillard's Technique' is from* Vuillard, témoignage *(Paris 1945). For a general introduction to the subject, M. Salomon's* Vuillard *(Gallimard, Paris 1968) can be strongly recommended to anyone who reads French.*

My first meeting with Vuillard took place in June 1920. I had been invited to dinner with K.-X. Roussel at L'Etang-la-Ville, and when I arrived I found him there chatting with his old friend under the shady trees of La Jaconnette.

I can still picture that wonderful garden of Roussel's as it first appeared to me then; it was as carefully composed as one of his paintings. From the road a rising path between lime trees led to a broad terrace from which, through the trees, one overlooked the beautiful stretch of country that is encircled by the forest of Marly. To the east, on a clear day, you could see Mont Valérien in the distance, and, beyond it, the Eiffel Tower and the white domes of Montmartre.

I had known Roussel for only a short time. Nobody until then had attracted me so swiftly and irresistibly; what was I going to think of his friend Vuillard?

Seen from a distance the two men were as unlike as possible. There was a direct contrast between the tall figure and highly individual distinction of Roussel, in his dove-grey velvet suit bespattered, here and there, with the ultramarine paint he used for his skies, and the short, formal, black-clad figure of Vuillard. He wore a small soft hat with turned-up brim, and a loose bow tie like a black dickey concealed by a near-white beard, cut square. He was smoking a small clay pipe that I never saw him with again. What struck me first was the expression of his keen, grave gaze, suddenly lit up by a really charming smile as soon as he held out his hand to me. I found it the most natural thing in the world to join in the conversation that had already been begun by the two friends. Once again experience showed me that beings of rare quality can be recognized immediately by an extreme simplicity which makes all sorts of contact possible.

In the friendliest way, Vuillard asked me about the journey I had recently made along the River Plate; but I soon brought the conversation back to painting, being too anxious to question him myself and get to the heart of what interested me. I remember how, that evening, he spoke to us at some length about Vouet and Le Sueur, with whose works, I admit to my shame, I was not well acquainted. When I asked a few discreet questions about the so-called experiments of modern painting, mentioning a few names that were in the news, I found him uninterested or unwilling to discuss the matter.

While our conversation went on, I was conscious of a growing sense of sympathy mingled with respect for this man, whose speech had an individual quality that delighted me; one seemed, as he spoke, to catch his thoughts in all their fresh warmth, expressed with scrupulous care.

After dinner we walked round the garden again until night fell and it was time to part. I was struck by the way the two friends clasped one another in a long embrace. Then Vuillard and I made our way slowly to the station, which stands on the other side of the village on the opposite hillside.

While we were waiting for the train Vuillard talked to me about his mother, with tenderness and reverence. He told me that she was expecting him at Vaucresson, in the little villa, La Closerie des Genêts, which he rented for the summer, not far from the Clos Cézanne where his friends the Hessels lived, and he invited me to visit him there quite soon. As the train came into the station he said, with a touching expression: 'Maman is my muse.'

I never forgot that confession: at our very first meeting Vuillard had revealed his secret. I think that in order to grasp the essential and deeply human quality of his work one must be aware of the tender adoration that Vuillard felt for his mother....

Vuillard first met Madame Hessel in 1900. And it was in her apartment in the rue de Rivoli that henceforward he found most of his sitters, the most constant of these being Madame Hessel herself.

It was on the day of my first visit to La Closerie des Genêts that I made her acquaintance. I had heard a great deal about her; I knew that she belonged to a brilliant social set and that she had long been Vuillard's close friend and consequently was almost one of the family. All this had aroused my keen curiosity. I had also heard that Tristan Bernard had nicknamed her 'Vuillard's Dragon'. I was reminded of this by the contrast between her tall figure and that of her friend. She had a fine presence and great elegance, and was a supremely gracious and accomplished hostess. Under her snow-white curly hair her black eyes had an expression of gentle sweetness which gave her great charm. We took to one another immediately, and in spite of her regret, which she artlessly expressed on our first acquaintance, at my not being Jewish, we formed solid bonds of friendship which became further strengthened with time.

Henceforward I became a constant witness to the deep mutual affection which bound Madame Hessel to Vuillard. For twenty years I went several times a week to sit before dinner in Madame Hessel's drawing-room in the rue de Naples, where I was sure of finding Vuillard; and I can recall to this day, with emotion, the confidential moments when we shared the delight of those conversations, often about mere trifles, which give life its sweetness. Against the walls, hung with beige velvet, paintings by Bonnard, Renoir and Degas formed an enchanted circle that glowed in the lamplight.

Often Vuillard and I got there first and waited for Madame Hessel, who was detained by her social duties. As soon as she appeared she and Vuillard would embrace one another fondly, while she asked after her friend's health; for he often suffered from hay fever. 'You're over-tired, Edouard,' she would say. Then, after inquiring after his mother, she would question him about his sitters: 'What, are you starting the Noailles portrait again? You'll never have done with it!' 'Well, Ingres spent nine years over Madame d'Haussonville,' Vuillard replied with a smile.

She often teased Vuillard about his lack of personal smartness. One evening she noticed that his trousers were worn quite threadbare over the knees. She flared up, declaring that he was quite impossible, that he put her to shame, and that she never wanted to see him again in the offending garment. Vuillard, in some embarrassment, tried laughingly to soothe her; I joined in, supporting one and defending the other. In the end Vuillard swore by all that was holy that he would become a well-dressed man. I can still see him swaying about in his armchair while Madame Hessel raised her eyes to heaven as though appealing to it to bear witness to this empty promise.

Vuillard always set great store by Madame Hessel's judgment and often, during the course of his work, would ask her to come and give her opinion.

Relations between Madame Hessel and Madame Vuillard were always perfectly amiable, but sometimes Madame Vuillard betrayed a touch of jealousy, interspersing her praises with a few malicious comments on the physical appearance of her rival: her height, or her chin, or her hands, which Madame Vuillard considered too big. They may have been, but they were very beautiful in my opinion, with the flexible fingers and the fine curves which Vuillard has so well portrayed.

The Hessels entertained a great deal, both in Paris, in the rue de Naples, and at Vaucresson, at the Clos Cézanne. One frequent visitor was Lucie Hessel's cousin Madame Aron, who later became Madame Tristan Bernard. She was extremely pretty, and Vuillard has hardly flattered her in the fine portrait he painted of her in 1914. Other visitors were Romain Coolus, André Picard, Alfred Natanson, Tristan Bernard, Yves Mirande, and Alfred Savoir and his wife. The latter, who was known as Miche, later married Léopold Marchand; Vuillard, who greatly appreciated her charm and sweet nature, often put her into his pictures. The Hessels' friends also included Léon Blum and his brother René, Marcel Kapferer, Jos Hessel's constant partner at poker, and Jean Laroche, the perfect gastronome. Both Kapferer and Laroche were great art collectors. Also to be met there were the enchanting Emmy Lunn, and sometimes Yvonne Printemps and Sacha Guitry.

Roussel was too independent in mind and character to have much in common with the Hessel set. His rare appearances invariably created a sensation, because of his strange and impressive personality. It was at his own home, with Bonnard, Maillol, Thadée Natanson, Vollard or Léon Werth, that he displayed his gifts to the full and delighted his friends.

Vuillard's constant presence at the Hessels' puzzled many people. His grave air, his apostolic face, his customary silence – everything about him seemed strange in that card-playing, gossiping company. But he was there because of his affection for Lucie Hessel. He found these social gatherings restful, and Madame Hessel's smile ensured his serenity. . . .

When I came to know Hessel, his position was well established although it had not yet reached its apogee. He was rightly held to be the ablest picture-dealer in Paris. His way of buying pictures was unique. Before even seeing the painting offered him, he would scowl discouragingly and declare it to be a fake or a horror; but as soon as he had acquired it he invariably described it as a masterpiece. Disdainful towards most people, he was very affable with his customers. He would sit all day in a great armchair beside the entrance to his shop, reading the papers, particularly the sporting news, weighing up the favourites' chances or, with closed eyes, concocting Machiavellian business deals. He was probably driven by a love of gambling, of taking risks, rather than by the thirst for gain. At the end of the day he would rush off to a game of poker, to keep up his reputation for being unlucky at cards. During the racing season, even if Hessel was at his country home, a book-maker would call every morning to take his bets.

Vuillard delighted in the stories about Hessel which went the rounds, and which eventually created a legend about him. He told me that when Hessel, in co-operation with the Bernheim brothers, was running their gallery, which had been moved to the avenue de l'Opéra, he would lay a bet with his cousins, at ten o'clock every morning, about the number of bearded men who would pass in the next quarter of an hour. They also laid bets on the number of cabs. In those days there were two principal cab companies in Paris: the Urbaine and the Parisienne. Their drivers wore top-hats of stiffened leather: those of the Urbaine were white, those of the Parisienne black. Bets were laid as soon as the shop opened. Hessel lost so regularly that he came to suspect that he was being swindled. Arriving earlier than usual one morning he caught one of his cousins bargaining, watch in hand, with a coachman to whom he had just handed a coin. That cat was out of the bag, and something else had to be thought up.

On several occasions I witnessed Hessel's method of selling a picture. His arguments varied little, but the repetition of the same well-chosen words invariably won the day. Once, in order to overcome the reluctance of an art collector on whom he was pressing a second-rate picture, Hessel offered to buy it back in six months' time, at the same price, if he did not like it, and the matter was settled. A few weeks went by, and the two men met again at a shooting-party lunch. At the very beginning of the meal, the collector told Hessel, jokingly, that he was definitely dissatisfied with the picture and reminded him of the conditions of the sale. Hessel replied that he was very willing to take the picture back. His eager satisfaction set the art lover wondering. At the end of the lunch he went up to Hessel to ask him when he would fetch the picture. 'Tomorrow morning,' Hessel replied. The other, decidedly intrigued, questioned Hessel, who told him: 'The day I sold you that painting, one of my customers who had seen it before you was so disappointed at missing it that he offered me fifty thousand francs more than I asked you, if I could get it back – so you've just made two people happy!' A few minutes later, the art collector changed his mind and handed Hessel a cheque for fifty thousand francs.

Vuillard seldom painted direct from nature; his pictures were almost always done from a sketch. He was constantly drawing his friends, and those who found his eye upon them knew that they must hold the pose in which he had caught them.

Vuillard's sketches are so interesting in relation to his finished work that I must speak about them here. Throughout his life Vuillard continually filled his notebooks with them, noting down everything that he saw during the day: his mother at breakfast, a bunch of flowers on a table, the view from his window, the corner of a street or of a garden, even effects of darkness or the vaulted ceiling of the Métro. Nothing failed to interest him, and his exceptional gift of draughtsmanship enabled him to record the most unexpected sights. These sketches are very summary, often akin to shorthand. Many of them are simply brief notations, indicating the essential proportions and character of a form or a detail. When he came home, Vuillard would transfer his drawing to a sheet of cardboard or a canvas, or more frequently to a piece of paper which he cut from a roll that stood permanently in one corner of his studio.

He would immediately proceed to paint, in oils or in colours mixed with glue (à la colle), and his astonishing memory would bring back to him the colour-relations which it had registered.

I can still picture Vuillard at a social gathering. He would suddenly look intently at a group or an object, not as painters usually do, considering the object that interests them with one eye closed or through narrowed lids so as to blur the details and bring out the essential points, but on the contrary with a direct stare. Then his face would grow grave, and without taking his eyes off his subjects he would whip his notebook out of his pocket, seize his Koh-i-Noor 5B, and, without hesitation, start to draw. He worked with great speed, scarcely glancing at his paper, entirely preoccupied by the sight before him, composing his picture from nature. He did not identify the objects in front of his eyes; his line ran round their shapes, suggested their contents, marked the accents, imposed order on his sensations. He did not separate things, he connected them. His work seemed to obey a secret agreement between the sight before him and his exquisite receptive faculties, so readily moved, an agreement that transported him into the poetic atmosphere indispensable for creation. In certain respects we might compare the artist's state of total absorption with the state of grace in which the worshipper at prayer uses words – just as Vuillard uses his pencil – only to reach an invisible world beyond, the realm of that pure love with which he is in communion. . . .

On my first visit to the rue de Calais, Vuillard was working on two portraits: that of the painter Baignières in his horizon-blue uniform, and that of Madame Val Synave, which is truly a masterpiece. It was the character of *inevitability* that struck me when I looked at these two paintings, which I could to a certain extent compare with nature, since their setting was Vuillard's studio. Apart from the strangeness of his way of painting *à la colle*, to which I was unaccustomed and whose rough texture surprised me, I could not conceive of any different way of painting. I think everyone feels that way about the work he loves. . . .

Everything seemed to become clear when one was in Vuillard's company; he was so well balanced, and he always brought things back to the essential point, with clarity and restraint. In discussions he liked to quote Marshal Foch's phrase *De quoi s'agit-il?* ('What's it all about?') Thoughtful, serious without ever being sententious, he enjoyed jokes and laughed over witticisms, although his own turn of mind did not lead him to make them. Kind and tolerant in all things, he showed severity only in his judgments on art.

His simple tastes, his unpretentious way of life, that spirit of charity that imbued all his words and actions – all impressed me deeply. I sometimes told him, jokingly so as not to offend his modesty, that he was a saint; he denied it with a smile. It was not only his goodness that made him akin to such exceptional beings, but also his humility and his unbounded tenderness. Like the pure in heart, he was in love with the beauty of the world, in a constant fashion and to the highest degree. Inspiration was latent in him. A meeting with a friend, something he had seen, the thought of someone dear to him, would bring a tear to his eyes; a minute later, concentration would bring something like severity to them. I lived in such close intimacy with him that it is only at this distance of time that I can see things as they really were, and become aware through his example of the mysterious intercourse that the artist maintains with the world. That intercourse constitutes his vocation.

Next to his gaze, of course, the most striking detail of his features was the redness of his lip which, when he smiled, gleamed red as a cherry under his thick, wavy moustache. This gave him a look of extreme youthfulness and revealed the sensuousness to which all his work bears witness. His deep, sonorous voice, with its great variety of tone and clear articulation, added an unforgettable charm to his conversation. . . .

It was a great treat for me whenever Vuillard invited me to lunch, particularly while his mother was alive, for she always contributed to our gatherings that gracious kindness which her son's friends had so much appreciated in their youth. After her death these family lunch parties became less frequent and lost much of their attraction.

On these occasions I generally arrived early so as to have some talk with Vuillard by himself. After having exchanged a few words with his mother, I would knock at the door of the studio drawing-room, and go in by myself, for she was tactfully reluctant to disturb her son. While painting, Vuillard often wore a long white smock which he pulled on over his head. In the excitement of his work he would wipe his brushes on it to get rid of excess paint, and so his sleeves and the front of his garment were bespattered with enchanting embellishments. While I sat in an armchair by the window and talked to him about all manner of things, he busied himself about his task, still smiling, coming and going between the easel and his pots of glue. 'I'm listening, I'm listening,' he would say if, seeing him at grips with some problem, I broke off my remarks.

Tables, chairs and floor were strewn with pages of sketches to which he paid close attention, consulting them almost before every brush-stroke. From time to time he would stop and take a few steps backward to consider the general effect of his picture. With bent head, peering keenly over his spectacles, a little pot of paint in one hand and his brush in the other, he would rub the groove between his moustaches with his free forefinger. Then, as though pressed for time, he would hurry back to his canvas, stir the pots on his stove to soften the paint which had thickened as it cooled, and mix his colours without appearing to determine their proportions, simply by dipping his wet brush into his powders. At last he would stop, collapse into his armchair – which he declared to be an indispensable piece of furniture for a painter – and meditate, with his eyes still fixed on his work. Then, suddenly getting up again, he would take a piece of charcoal or pastel to recover some shape which he had lost. Sometimes he had recourse to the squares which he traced on his canvas with a ruler; armed with a magnifying-glass, he would examine his sketch through the squares on his tracing-paper. I must not forget to mention among the implements used by Vuillard the indispensable and enchanting little multicoloured feather duster with which he removed the excess charcoal on his canvas before resuming his painting *à la colle*.

I was witness to the difficulties he encountered about the position of the legs in the portrait of the Comtesse de Polignac; how many times he began them over again! The great simplicity of our relationship sometimes emboldened me to make certain comments. One day, seeing him go back yet again over that part of his picture which, overloaded with paint, was beginning to show cracks, I told him my opinion. No doubt I anticipated his own intention, for the moment after he soaked the whole lower part of his canvas with hot water and began to scratch it boldly with a penknife.

When I teased him about these incrustations of paint which, it seemed to me, might endanger the survival of his work, he would reply with perfect confidence that his painting would, on the contrary, become as hard as rock. 'That may be,' I would say, 'but those cracks which you seem so fond of will be real dust-traps.' 'You'll only have to blow on them,' he would say, 'and rub them with breadcrumb.' The fact is that these paintings *à la colle* have all been preserved in a state of perfect freshness. Witness for instance the decorations in the foyer of the Comédie des Champs-Elysées: these have been exposed, without glass, ever since 1913, to the overheated atmosphere of a theatre with its tobacco smoke and dust.

At the first signal telling us that lunch was served Vuillard would whip off his smock, go to wash his hands and promptly join us in the dining-room. Madame Vuillard's linen and silver were of the finest quality and I remember those beautiful white napkins with large embroidered initials which, being too heavily starched, kept slipping off one's knees under the table. The *plat de résistance* was often roast chicken with pork crackling, a succulent dish over which Madame Vuillard took particular care. I invariably did it full justice. Vuillard, without being greedy, had a hearty appetite and he, too, appreciated good cooking.

Apart from the family, Dr Parvu, Vaquez's assistant, who was so devoted to Madame Vuillard and who appears in several paintings, was often one of the party. Of Romanian origin but very much a Parisian, he mixed a great deal with theatrical people. He had been De Max's friend and was Cécile Sorel's doctor, and his conversation was always lively and unconventional.

After lunch we would go for coffee into the studio drawing-room and carry on our conversation, sometimes very late, particularly when Roussel was of the party and Vuillard had no sitters expecting him.

I remember the traditional phrase with which the ladies, after a short while, would take leave of us: 'We'll let the gentlemen talk about painting'. What did 'talk about painting' mean for them – or for the uninitiated in general, who have no inkling that the conversation of artists is really a lovers' dialogue, in which silences abound and a word, an allusion to some particular work, sets each of them rapturously daydreaming? To talk about painting means, for painters, to share the same enthusiasms in intimate communion, to reach agreement on their various reasons for loving the same works of art, to enjoy the inexpressible together.

I remember that one day, after we had been talking at some length about a work with which we were very familiar, we found ourselves at variance over an important detail of the subject represented. I can still picture Roussel's thumb sketching the shape in question on his knee, whereas Vuillard and I had a different recollection of it. After having resorted to our pencils, we were obliged to refer to the photographic reproduction, which decided the question. This suggests that what moves us in a picture is less the thing depicted than something indefinable, and that the works which have the greatest hold over our minds may be those whose subject evades us.

Apart from these gatherings, in which Madame Vuillard participated discreetly, my affection for her impelled me to pay her frequent visits. I went by preference in the evenings, about six o'clock, when I knew that she would be alone and glad to see me. I sometimes found her at the piano, which she played, so she would say, not so much for the sake of the music as to unstiffen her fingers. More frequently, she would be doing her embroidery at a table covered with a dark red cloth, under

Interior with a Lady and a Dog   1910

XVI   The Black Cups (Misia Sert and her Niece)   1919–24

II Sketch for Portrait of Pierre Bonnard *c*. 1925

XVIII In the Park at Les Clayes *c.* 1936

a hanging lamp with a yellow shade. She called me her 'little stepson'. I remember, too, being bothered by the lighted lamp on the piano behind her, whose reflector dazzled me, so that after a few moments I would invariably get up to turn it out. What interested me was not so much the stories she told about her long life as the way she talked about people. She was a keen observer, and excelled at judging all the various people she had met thanks to her son. Intuitively she gauged their good qualities and made fun of their failings with the alert wit of an old Parisienne who is not to be taken in by appearances.

One evening I found her in company with Yvonne Printemps, who had come to bring her the flowers that had been sent to her dressing-room on the first night of a new play. There was an amusing contrast between the charming little old lady in her lace cap and the elegant actress, swathed in furs, covered with diamonds and heavily scented, lavishing compliments and endearments; each of them seemed somewhat self-conscious and made great efforts to be charming to the other. 'Of course,' Madame Vuillard said to me after she had left, nodding towards the magnificent basket of flowers, 'all this isn't for me. It's for Edouard.' She was flattered none the less, and appreciated the consideration paid her by her son's friends. . . .

If one had to trace Vuillard's antecedents, I suppose the first name to occur to one would be that of Degas. Like Degas, Vuillard always took his subjects from Parisian life. He, too, chronicled his own time, although in different social settings; like Degas, he composed his pictures from nature, using direct sketches, and constantly searching for new methods and techniques. Each of them was a severe critic and contemptuous of easily achieved successes. More sociable than his senior, Vuillard none the less managed, like Degas, to protect himself from curiosity by taking as little part as possible in public life. It was only on the pressing and tireless entreaties of Maurice Denis and David-Weill – in order not to offend them and also, I have no hesitation in saying, out of humility – that Vuillard consented in 1937 to enter the Institut. He was hurt by the ungenerous interpretations to which his election gave rise.

The painters whose names recurred most frequently in Vuillard's conversation were perhaps Puvis de Chavannes, Corot and Delacroix. Some people may wonder at his admiration for Puvis. Yet we should consider how close are the delicate, almost grisaille tints dear to the painter of the *Life of St Genevieve* to the narrow range of harmonies in which Vuillard delighted. Puvis's methods of work, moreover, provided Vuillard with constant and valuable lessons. . . .

One morning, round about 1930, I called at Vuillard's before lunch. His maid informed me that Monsieur had gone out early and would not be back before late that evening. I was intrigued, and put some tactful questions to Marie, who was so loyally devoted to her master but suffered from his oppressive silences. 'You know, monsieur,' she said resignedly, 'that Monsieur never tells me anything about what he's doing.' Then, after a pause: 'But he may perhaps have gone to Amiens, like last time.' That 'last time' had been several years previously. And in fact Vuillard, seized with a sudden desire for another look at *Ludus pro Patria*, had gone off to spend the day by himself at Amiens. At the top of the museum staircase, opposite these pictures, all the preliminary drawings made by Puvis are exhibited in groups that enable one to see clearly in what way the artist worked when transposing his notes and sketches.

It was in order to stress their common origin as natives of the Jura that Vuillard one day, as a joke, drew his self-portrait in the likeness of Puvis.

Vuillard was very fond of Corot; it amused him to think that both of them had grown up with a dressmaker's workroom not far away. In his frequent visits to the Louvre he seldom failed to pause before the *Interior of Sens Cathedral* or the *Belfry of Douai*, which he regarded as masterpieces. He always had in front of him a very fine photograph of Corot in old age. As I commented one day on the touching expression of kindliness in that rugged face: 'Don't you believe it,' he said. 'Look at the mischievous look in his eyes!' – implying thereby that it takes more than a kind heart to make a good painter.

Vuillard often lingered thoughtfully in the Chapelle des Anges in Saint-Sulpice, before the admirable mural paintings by Delacroix, which he considered among the greatest masterpieces of their kind. In this connection he maintained that great artists always produced their finest works in their maturity. Delacroix's *Journal*, *Letters* and writings on painters were among Vuillard's favourite reading.

I remember that one winter, when he was housebound, Vuillard became enthusiastic over George Sand's *Consuelo*, which he read on the recommendation of Alain, who was at that time a friend of Roussel's. Certain reflections on art, which occur in this appealing book, delighted him, and they seemed to him so true and so penetrating that he felt they must reflect the conversations which George Sand had had with Delacroix.

He always felt a special gratitude towards Monet, who had recognized and encouraged him from the beginning. Towards 1920 the painter of the *Nymphéas* had begun to fall into undeserved ill-favour; it was at the beginning of the reaction against Impressionism. Vuillard repeatedly went to visit him at Giverny in token of his undiminished admiration. One fine spring morning I went there with Roussel and Vuillard, whom Monet had asked to lunch. Monet came to meet us at the gate and insisted on inviting Annette and myself to join the party. It was an unforgettable occasion, every detail of which is still clear in my mind.

After a splendid meal, which included the traditional *canard au feu d'enfer*, the final touches to which were delicately performed at table, before our eyes, by Monet himself, and before continuing our visit round that magical garden with its water-lily pond, we took coffee in the little studio drawing-room. My mind was so alert that day that I could, even now, describe the scene and repeat Monet's remarks and the sallies and anecdotes which studded the unpretentious conversation of these three great artists. I can still hear Monet say about Sisley: 'What a lovely painter!' and Vuillard, without a trace of flattery: 'Yes, but he can't draw like you,' – and Monet agreeing with an imperceptible nod. On the wall before us an unframed canvas, almost bare but for a few masterly brush-strokes, seemed to prove the point. Roussel looked at it unceasingly. I could read his thoughts in his eyes; and then he suddenly exclaimed, with that highly individual intonation of his, and with a little laugh as though apologizing for the vehement sincerity of his words: 'Monet, you're a Greek!' and everyone fell silent.

I think Vuillard placed Rembrandt highest of all; but his eclecticism allowed him to take an interest in the most diverse achievements.

Sometimes I accompanied him to the Louvre. From the very first days of our acquaintance, he asked me to pose for him in the Salle des Cariatides with a view to certain panels he had been commissioned to paint for Basle, whose subjects were to be Sculpture and Painting. I still remember the calf of a certain antique statue over which, one morning, he lingered with me for a long time.

On another occasion, we stood looking at Rigaud's portraits. 'What a painter! Did you know that Rigaud had a studio in which he employed a number of pupils? Some of them painted draperies, others cuirasses or swords, each of them had his own speciality; but he, Rigaud, only painted the heads – and he would finish a head in a single day! What wonderful teamwork, and what knowledge of his craft!'

I remember, too, how we paused in front of Prud'hon's portrait of Joséphine de Beauharnais, and he praised its grace and skilful modelling. But his most constant admiration, I thought, was for Le Sueur. How often he made me admire the *Gathering of Artists round a Table*, and the *Scenes from the Life of St Bruno*! 'Look at the colour values in that hand against the background,' he would say, pointing to the figure of Raymond Diocres preaching from his lofty pulpit, 'and what fine painting in the shadows!' Further on, when we came to the *Muses* of the Hôtel Lambert decorations: 'Look at those delightful Parisian faces! Like Renoir's models!' And again: 'What craftsmanship these people had!'

This question of craftsmanship preoccupied Vuillard constantly, and he often recalled the anxious days of his youth, when he lacked the support which earlier generations of painters found at the onset of their careers. But should we not appreciate the merits of that regenerative empiricism to which Vuillard and his companions were obliged to have recourse?

Jacques Salomon
Vuillard's Technique

During the twenty years of my intimate acquaintance with Vuillard, his modesty and simplicity made our relations so informal that it never occurred to me that I might one day decide to give a personal account of him, and I am sorry today that I never took notes on our conversations.

It so happens that of all his friends I was the one who, on account both of my love for painting, and of the family connections between us, was most truly initiated into the secrets of his work, his researches, his technique. In another age I could have called him my master. I have tried in these pages to shed some light on Vuillard as man and as artist. I have shown him at work; it now remains to speak of his technique.

I should like to dwell on two aspects of his work which require a certain elucidation: his paintings on cardboard and his method of painting *à la colle*, with glue.

If Vuillard at the outset of his career painted on cardboard, it was primarily for reasons of economy. His first attempts were made on the bottoms of boxes from his mother's workroom. He remained faithful to this type of support for a long time, both for the sake of its absorbent qualities and because of the ochre or grey tone which it provided as a base for his colour harmonies; later he used tinted paper for this latter purpose.

Most of the time Vuillard painted in oil on 'unprepared' cardboard such as is found in ordinary commercial use. His pictures were almost always swiftly executed without retouching; they present a matt surface, since the oil mixed with the colours has sunk into the cardboard and the spirit used to dilute them has evaporated.

Collectors and dealers should be warned that they are inviting disaster if they rashly attempt to varnish these paintings on cardboard with a view to making them brighter.

If the cardboard is entirely covered with paint there is, of course, no danger in varnishing the picture. This can be tested by passing a damp sponge over the painting: where the colour has not penetrated, spots will appear which will vanish on evaporation.

If on the other hand Vuillard has left areas where the cardboard is exposed, as is most frequently the case, the effect of varnish will be disastrous: since varnish does not evaporate on drying, it will leave brown patches on the unpainted parts of the picture and ruin the harmony of the whole.

Imprudent art lovers often came shamefacedly to confess their misadventures to Vuillard; the damage was irreparable.

Occasionally, in order to make his cardboard less absorbent, Vuillard covered it with a light coat of pure glue. In this case the unpainted parts present a faintly shiny appearance which is due to the fine film formed by the glue as it dried. This film protects the cardboard and allows the picture to be varnished without risk.

There is a third case: Vuillard sometimes prepared his picture with a layer of glue mixed with powdered colour in order to give his support the local tints he required. This presents the same disadvantage as untreated cardboard, since in this case the powder, although mixed with glue, absorbs the varnish and turns dark.

The best way to show these paintings to advantage is to cover them with a sheet of glass, which will take the place of varnish and at the same time will protect them from dust.

Let us now consider the technique of painting *à la colle*, which is a sort of distemper painting and akin to fresco. In fresco, a word which in Italian simply means 'fresh', the artist paints with powdered colours diluted in water, which he spreads rapidly on a newly plastered wall. Once the wall has dried no alteration is possible. Glue-painting, on the other hand, allows an unlimited amount of retouching and modifying.

If Vuillard very often made use of this method, which he had discovered as a young man, it was primarily, as in the case of cardboard, for reasons of economy. But, once used to it, he came to love it and eventually acquired great virtuosity in it. He did not invent this process, which has always been used by scene-painters and also by many eighteenth-century decorative artists when they painted panels or screens. His originality consists in the exceptional feat of using glue for works which seem akin to straightforward oil painting.

We may wonder, at least in the case of the great interiors painted during his last twenty-five years, why Vuillard used this distemper process to do what he could have done more swiftly, and on the whole more conveniently, with oils. Distemper as he practised it demanded an elaborate apparatus: a spirit lamp or electric stove, quantities of pots and pans, a host of boxes and bags of powdered colour. But not only did Vuillard prize the matt tones obtained by this method of painting: he considered that this refractory process helped him to keep his excessive facility under control, and allowed him to deliberate more fully over his work, if only during the pauses while his colours were drying. It provided him with many an unforeseen discovery: and above all it allowed him to go on experimenting, transforming and retouching almost *ad infinitum*.

Let us examine his *cuisine* in greater detail. The glue used by Vuillard was not quite the same as that used by scene-painters, which is a sort of sticky gelatine known as size, which they dissolve in three or four times its own volume of warm water. It lasts only a few days and goes bad very quickly. Vuillard preferred Tottin glue, which is sold in brownish sheets at colourmen's shops. In default of this, I have seen him use ordinary cabinet-makers' glue, which is as brown as caramel. These sheets are left to soak for twelve hours, at the end of which they become limp and swell up: they are then dissolved in a *bain-marie* in four or five times their volume of water, and the medium is ready for use.

When he had a large surface to cover, Vuillard would prepare his colours beforehand in pots of suitable size, mixing his powders as the fancy took him and keeping them constantly warm in the *bain-marie* to prevent them from thickening.

When applying colour to cardboard, canvas or paper the artist must take into account the fact that it will grow lighter when the water has evaporated. Vuillard paid close attention to this change, which took from five to fifteen minutes, depending on the temperature of the room in which he was working and the thickness of the layers of paint already applied; and he modified his colours accordingly. This is what I meant when I spoke of 'unforeseen discoveries'. In changing before his eyes a colour could at a given moment acquire a nuance unimaginable before; Vuillard would then have to remix his colours to reconstitute that nuance.

Sometimes it took him hours to reconstitute a colour which he had put on the painting and no longer had to hand; either to harmonize with what was already part of the picture, or to get back to his original outlines, Vuillard would work over the area in question until it was literally encrusted with paint.

In order to avoid this laborious experimentation on his canvas, he would often lay out his tints on whatever scrap of paper was within reach. He dried them rapidly by holding them over the red-hot wires of his electric fire. He would then examine them attentively, thus continuing in another field, as he said, the process of matching colours which had been practised by his grandfather Michaud, a textile manufacturer at Fresnoy-le-Grand. It was from him that he claimed to have inherited his sensitivity to nuances.

Often, as the water evaporated, his glue would thicken and get sticky; but, when carried away by his work, he would use it as it was, delighted with a *matière* which became, as he said, hard as rock, even cracking when he laid it on over layers which had not had time to dry. This could seriously damage an oil painting, but it does not injure painting *à la colle*, since the water with which the glue is impregnated, more innocuous than oil, evaporates quickly.

Sometimes, when confronted with veritable humps of paint which, when lit obliquely, deformed the face in a portrait, Vuillard was reduced to soaking the thickest passages of paint with warm water and then scraping them with a knife; when it dried, that area of the painting sometimes recovered a simplicity and tonal quality which he had long sought for in vain.

With such a method, we cannot be surprised that he took a very long time to complete some of his large portraits. It would seem clear that his case was unique, and that no one else has ever used warm glue for this sort of work.

Needless to say, such paintings should never be varnished: but they should be protected from their great enemy, which is damp.

Glass will keep them free from dust. If, however, in course of time some should creep in, the picture can be cleaned with breadcrumb or a soft rubber.

Whereas an oil painting grows continuously and irremediably darker, as a result of air and varnish, painting *à la colle*, which dries almost instantaneously, undergoes no further transformation and will maintain its original colour indefinitely.

1   Still-life with Bottle and Carafe *c.* 1888

2 Dinner Time 1889

3 Self-portrait in a Straw Hat *c.* 1890

4 The Goose 1891

5 Two Little Girls 1891

7 Self-portrait in a Straw Hat *c.* 1892

8 Self-portrait *c.* 1892

9 Self-portrait *c.* 1892

10   Woman Sweeping   *c.* 1892

11   The Elegant Lady   *c.* 1892 (not illustrated)

13 The Kitchen 1892

26   Jeanne Raunay in *Iphigénie*   *c.* 1893

27   Stage Scene (possibly from Maeterlinck's *Pelléas et Mélisande*) *c.* 1893

28 Picnic *c.* 1898

E. Vuillard

36 Woman in an Interior *c.* 1895

37 Woman Seated in a Garden *c.* 1896

38　The Manicure　*c.* 1896

39 Misia at the Piano and Cipa Listening *c.* 1897

40 In the Garden *c.* 1895–98

41 Luncheon at Villeneuve-sur-Yonne
    (Misia with her Brother Cipa Godebski) 1897

42 Misia in the Fields *c.* 1898

43 The Attic Room 1897

44 The Family in the Garden 1898

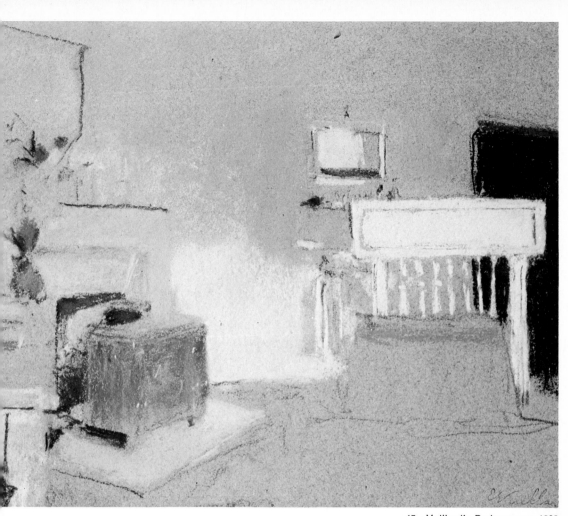

45 Vuillard's Bedroom *c.* 1898

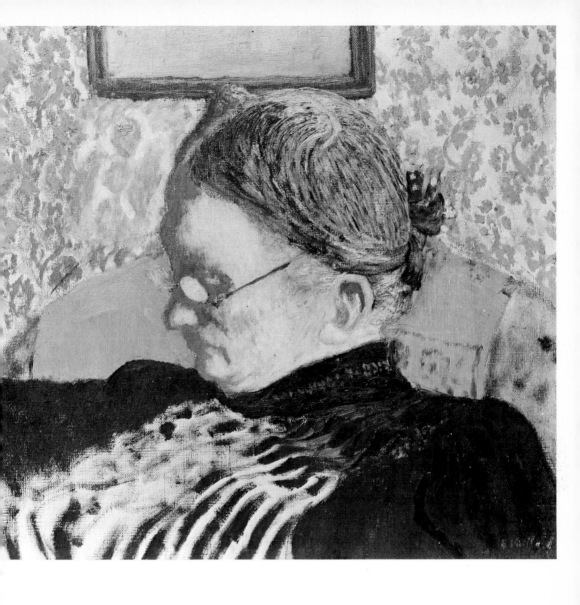

47 Vuillard's Mother in Profile *c.* 1898

48   Interior with Mother and Child   1899–1900

49 At the Window *c.* 1900

50   Window on Lac Léman   1900

51 The Red Roof 1900

52 Downhill View Towards a Garden *c.* 1900

53 Félix Vallotton *c.* 1900

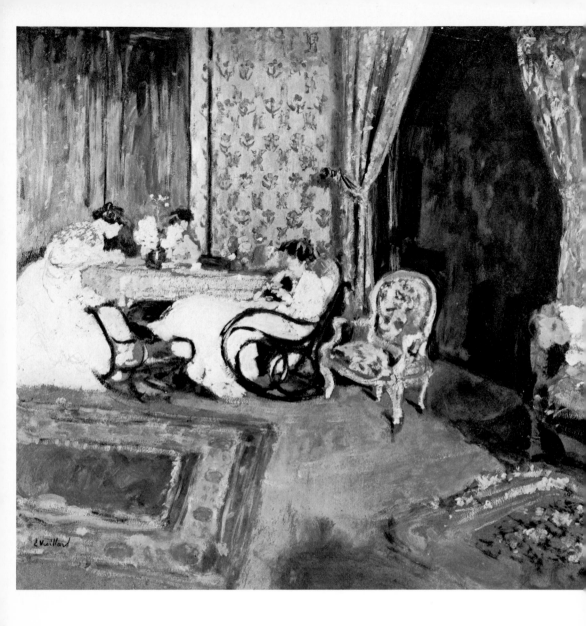

54 Women in an Interior   *c.* 1900

55 Interior   1900 (not illustrated)

57 Self-portrait 1903

58 Interior *c.* **1904**

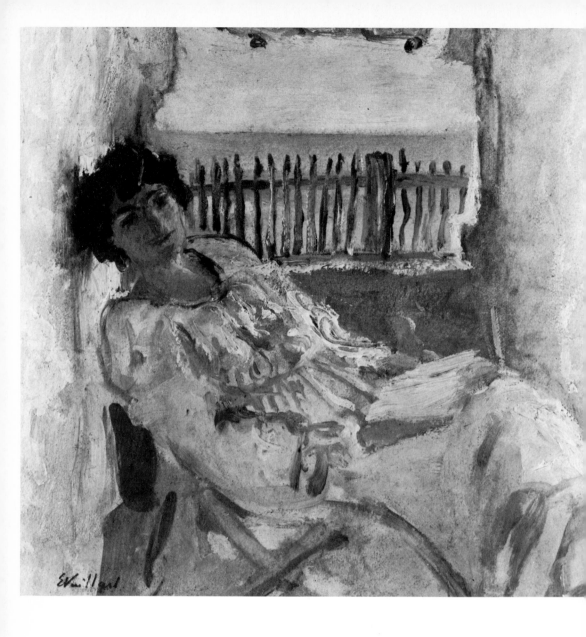

59 **At the Seashore (Lucie Hessel by the Sea)** *c.* 1904

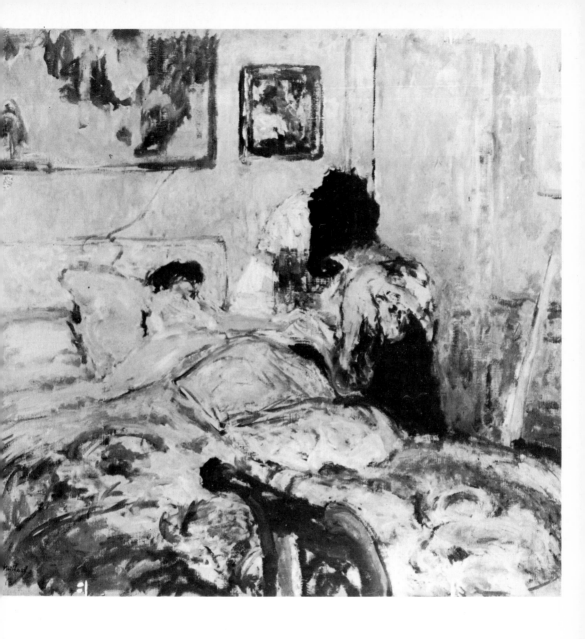

60　The Bedroom　*c.* 1905

61 Interior with Seated Woman 1904–05

65   View from the Artist's Studio, rue de la Pompe   *c.* 1905

67, 68 Studies for 'Place Vintimille' *c.* 1906

69 Rue Lepic, Paris *c.* 1908

70 Place Vintimille *c.* 1908

71 The Art Dealers *c.* 1908

73   Breton Coast, Pouliguen Lighthouse   *c.* 1908

74   The Saltings   *c.* 1910

75 Interior: Woman on a Sofa *c.* 1910

76   View on the Binnenalster, Hamburg   *c.* 1913

Mme Vuillard and Annette (In the Drawing-room)   1915–16

The Drawing-room, rue de Calais   *c.* 1918

80   The Salle des Cariatides at the Louvre   *c.* 1918

81   Study for 'The Salle des Cariatides at the Louvre'   *c.* 1918

82 The Salle des Cariatides at the Louvre (detail) *c.* 1918

83 Annette Dreaming *c.* 1918

84 Study for 'Mme Val Synave' 1920

85 Mme Val Synave 1920

86 The Sunny Room (Mme Vuillard's Room at Vaucresson) *c.* 1920

87 Dr Vaquez at the Hôpital Saint-Antoine *c*. 1921

88 Vuillard Washing his Hands *c.* 1921–25

89   Mme Vuillard Lighting her Stove   *c.* 1924

Mme Hessel   1924

Mme Gillou at Home   1931

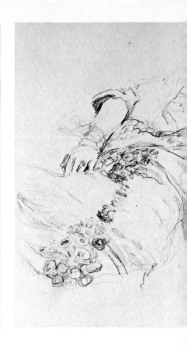

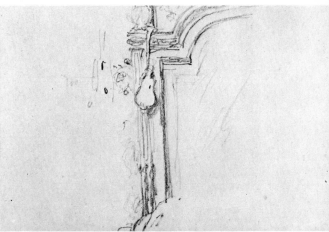

92–98   Seven Studies for
       'Anna de Noailles' *c.* 1932

99   Study for 'Anna de Noailles'
     c. 1932

100 Anna de Noailles *c.* 1932

102   Interior with a Lady Sewing   *c.* 1935

3   Cover to 'Landscapes and Interiors' series   1899

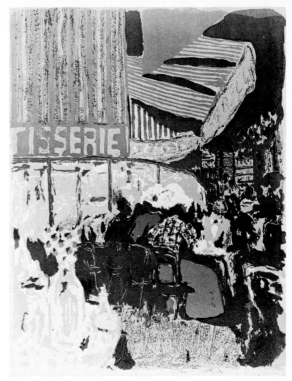

104   Cake for Tea   1899

105   On the Pont de l'Europe   1899

106 Pink Interior III 1899

107 Interior with Hanging Lamp 1899

108 Pink Interior I 1899

109 Pink Interior II 1899

110 The Fireplace 1899

111 The Cook 1899

112 The Game of Checkers 1899

113 The Two Sisters-in-law 1899

114   Across the Fields   1899

115   The Avenue   1899

Short Reading List

List of Illustrations

Short Reading List

The principal source of information about Vuillard in English has long been the catalogue, by Andrew Carnduff Ritchie and William S. Lieberman, for the exhibition organized in 1953 by the Museum of Modern Art in New York. This can still be read with profit, and the bibliography by Bernard Karpel is a model of its kind. The English edition (1946) of Claude Roger-Marx's *Vuillard: his Life and Work* has long been out of print. Salient articles in English include André Chastel's 'Vuillard' in *Art News Annual* (New York, 1954), Jacques Salomon's 'Vuillard Paints a Portrait' in *Art News Annual* (New York, 1962), and James Dugdale's two articles on 'Vuillard, the Decorator' in *Apollo* (London, February 1965 and October 1967). Mr Dugdale has also published *Vuillard* in 'The Masters' series (no. 97, London, 1967).

Indispensable books in French include four by Jacques Salomon: *Vuillard, témoignage* (Paris, Albin Michel, 1945); *Auprès de Vuillard* (Paris, La Palme, 1953); *Vuillard admiré* (Lausanne, La Bibliothèque des Arts, 1961); and *Vuillard* (Paris, Gallimard, 1968). André Chastel's *Vuillard, 1868–1940* (Paris, 1946) should be read in conjunction with his article 'Vuillard et Mallarmé' in *La Nef* (no. 26, January 1947). Claude Roger-Marx's *L'Œuvre gravé de Vuillard* (Monte Carlo, A. Sauret, 1948) presents a complete catalogue of the graphic work.

Among recent exhibition catalogues, that of 'Edouard Vuillard, K.-X. Roussel' at the Orangerie des Tuileries (Paris, 1968) is the most considerable; it is, in fact, as important for the documentation assembled by Jacques and Antoine Salomon and Pierre Georgel as it is for its two hundred and more illustrations.

List of Illustrations

This list embodies a catalogue of the exhibition 'Edouard Vuillard 1868–1940', shown between September 1971 and March 1972 at the Art Gallery of Ontario in Toronto, the California Palace of the Legion of Honor in San Francisco, and the Art Institute of Chicago.

Measurements are given in inches and centimetres, height before width. In the Graphic Works section the numbers prefixed by 'CRM' refer to Claude Roger-Marx's catalogue. Thanks are due to Lumley-Cazalet Ltd, London, for help with material for this section.

Decorative Schemes
not in exhibition

FOR CLAUDE ANET (p. 33)
In Front of the House   1898
Devant la maison
A la colle on canvas $84\frac{1}{4} \times 63\frac{3}{8}$ (214 × 161)
The Hon. James Dugdale, Yorkshire

In the Garden   1898
Dans le jardin
A la colle on canvas $84\frac{1}{4} \times 63\frac{3}{8}$ (214 × 161)
The Hon. James Dugdale, Yorkshire

FOR PAUL DESMARAIS (pp. 34–35)

Stroking the Dog   1892
La caresse au chien
Oil on canvas $189 \times 393\frac{3}{4}$ (485 × 1170)
Private collection, Paris

A Dressmaker's Workshop   1892
Un atelier de couture
Oil on canvas $189 \times 393\frac{3}{4}$ (485 × 1170)
Private collection, Paris

A Game of Badminton   1892
Une partie de volant
Oil on canvas $189 \times 393\frac{3}{4}$ (485 × 1170)
Private collection, Paris

Gardening   1892
Le jardinage
Oil on canvas $189 \times 393\frac{3}{4}$ (485 × 1170)
Private collection, Paris

A Dressmaker's Workshop II   1892
Un atelier de couture II
Oil on canvas $189 \times 393\frac{3}{4}$ (485 × 1170)
Private collection, Paris

Nursemaids and Children in a Public Garden   1892
Nourrices et enfants dans un jardin public
Oil on canvas $189 \times 393\frac{3}{4}$ (485 × 1170)
Private collection, Paris

THE PUBLIC GARDEN (pp. 36–39)

Out Walking 1894
La promenade
A la colle on canvas $83\frac{1}{2} \times 37\frac{3}{4}$ (212×96)
Museum of Fine Arts, Houston, Texas

Asking Questions 1894
L'interrogation
A la colle on canvas $83\frac{1}{2} \times 37\frac{3}{4}$ (212×96)
Present owner unknown

The Nursemaids 1894
Les nourrices
A la colle on canvas $83\frac{1}{2} \times 28\frac{3}{8}$ (212×72)
Musée National d'Art Moderne, Paris

Little Girls Playing 1894
Fillettes jouant
A la colle on canvas $83\frac{1}{2} \times 33\frac{1}{8}$ (212×84)
Present owner unknown

The First Steps 1894
Les premiers pas
A la colle on canvas $83\frac{1}{2} \times 26\frac{3}{8}$ (212×67)
Present owner unknown

The Conversation (Women on a Bench) 1894
La conversation (Femmes sur un banc)
A la colle on canvas $83\frac{1}{2} \times 59\frac{7}{8}$ (212×152)
Musée National d'Art Moderne, Paris

The Red Sunshade 1894
L'ombrelle rouge
A la colle on canvas $83\frac{1}{2} \times 31\frac{1}{2}$ (212×80)
Musée National d'Art Moderne, Paris

Under the Trees 1894
Sous les arbres
A la colle on canvas $83\frac{1}{2} \times 37\frac{3}{4}$ (212×96)
Cleveland Museum of Art

The Two Schoolboys 1894
Les deux écoliers
A la colle on canvas $83\frac{1}{2} \times 37\frac{3}{4}$ (212×96)
Musées Royaux des Beaux-Arts de Belgique, Brussels

PEOPLE IN ROOMS (pp. 40–41)

Music 1896
La musique
A la colle on canvas $826\frac{7}{8} \times 602\frac{1}{2}$ (2100×1530)
Musée du Petit Palais, Paris

The Library 1896
La bibliothèque
A la colle on canvas $826\frac{7}{8} \times 295\frac{1}{4}$ (2100×750)
Musée du Petit Palais, Paris

Dressmaking 1896
La couture
A la colle on canvas $826\frac{7}{8} \times 295\frac{1}{4}$ (2100×750)
Musée du Petit Palais, Paris

The Drawing-room 1896
Le salon
A la colle on canvas $826\frac{7}{8} \times 602\frac{1}{2}$ (2100×1530)
Musée du Petit Palais, Paris

THE COMÉDIE DES CHAMPS-ÉLYSÉES, PARIS
(pp. 42–45)

Scene from Le Malade Imaginaire by Molière 1912
Scène du Malade Imaginaire de Molière
A la colle on canvas $74 \times 120\frac{1}{8}$ (188×305)

Marthe Mellot in her Dressing-room 1912
Marthe Mellot dans sa loge
A la colle on canvas $22 \times 25\frac{5}{8}$ (56×65)

Lugné-Poe in his Dressing-room 1912
Lugné-Poe dans sa loge
A la colle on canvas $22 \times 25\frac{5}{8}$ (56×65)

The Puppet Show on the Champs-Elysées 1912
Guignol aux Champs-Elysées
A la colle on canvas $70 \times 20\frac{7}{8}$ (178×53)

Scene from Le Petit Café by Tristan Bernard 1912
Scène de Le Petit Café de Tristan Bernard
A la colle on canvas $74 \times 114\frac{1}{4}$ (188×290)

Bouquets of Flowers and Theatrical Posters 1912
Bouquets de fleurs et affiches de théâtre
A la colle on canvas One subject $21\frac{5}{8} \times 118\frac{1}{8}$ (55 × 300); two subjects each $21\frac{5}{8} \times 55\frac{1}{8}$ (55 × 140)

Scene from Massenet's opera *Grisélidis*(?) 1912
Scène de l'opéra *Grisélidis* de Massenet(?)
A la colle on canvas $88\frac{5}{8} \times 51\frac{1}{4}$ (225 × 130)

Scene from Debussy's opera *Pelléas et Mélisande* 1912
Scène de l'opéra *Pelléas et Mélisande* de Debussy
A la colle on canvas $88\frac{5}{8} \times 51\frac{1}{4}$ (225 × 130)

AT THE LOUVRE (pp. 46–47)

The Salle des Caryatides 1921
La salle des Caryatides
A la colle on canvas $63 \times 51\frac{1}{4}$ (160 × 130)
Bauer-Judlin collection, Binningen, near Basle

The Salle La Caze 1921
La salle La Caze
A la colle on canvas $63 \times 51\frac{1}{4}$ (160 × 130)
Bauer-Judlin collection, Binningen, near Basle

The Salle Clarac 1922
La salle Clarac
A la colle on canvas $38\frac{1}{4} \times 45\frac{1}{4}$ (97 × 115)
Bauer-Judlin collection, Binningen, near Basle

Vuillard's Chimneypiece 1922
La cheminée de Vuillard
A la colle on canvas $17\frac{3}{4} \times 45\frac{1}{4}$ (45 × 115)
Bauer-Judlin collection, Binningen, near Basle

A Statuette on Vuillard's Chimneypiece 1922
Statuette sur la cheminée de Vuillard
A la colle on canvas $17\frac{3}{4} \times 45\frac{1}{4}$ (45 × 115)
Bauer-Judlin collection, Binningen, near Basle

The Department of Sculpture at the Louvre 1922
Le Département de Sculpture au Louvre
A la colle on canvas $38\frac{1}{4} \times 45\frac{1}{4}$ (97 × 115)
Bauer-Judlin collection, Binningen, near Basle

PLACE VINTIMILLE (p. 48)

Place Vintimille 1 1907–08
A la colle on canvas $76\frac{3}{4} \times 25\frac{5}{8}$ (195 × 65)
Solomon R. Guggenheim Museum, New York

Place Vintimille 2 1907–08
A la colle on canvas $76\frac{3}{4} \times 25\frac{5}{8}$ (195 × 65)
Solomon R. Guggenheim Museum, New York

Easel Paintings and Studies
in exhibition except where otherwise indicated

I–XVIII ILLUSTRATED IN COLOUR (pp. 81–135)

I   The Dockers *c.* 1890
    Les débardeurs
    Oil on canvas
    $18\frac{1}{2} \times 24\frac{1}{2}$ (47 × 64)
    Mr and Mrs Arthur G. Altschul, New York

II The Landing, rue de Miromesnil 1891
    Le palier, rue de Miromesnil
    Oil on canvas
    9 × 16 approx. (33 × 24)
    Mrs Samuel Godfrey, Toronto

III An Outspoken Dinner Party (After the Meal) *c.* 1891
    Le dîner vert (Après le repas)
    Oil on canvas
    $13\frac{1}{4} \times 19\frac{3}{4}$ (34 × 49)
    The Hon. John Montagu, London

IV Lilacs 1892
    Lilas
    Oil on cardboard
    $14 \times 11\frac{1}{8}$ (35 × 28)

Mr and Mrs Donald S. Stralem,
New York

V   The Lady in Blue   *c.* 1894
La dame en bleu
Oil on cardboard
$19\frac{1}{4} \times 22\frac{7}{8}$ (49 × 58)
Private collection, Paris

VI   The Salon with Three Lamps,
rue Saint-Florentin   1899
Le salon aux trois lampes,
rue Saint-Florentin
Oil on canvas
$22\frac{7}{8} \times 37$ (58 × 94)
Gustav Zumsteg, Zürich

VII   Mother and Child   *c.* 1899
Mère et enfant
Oil on cardboard on wood
$19\frac{1}{8} \times 22\frac{1}{4}$ (48·5 × 56·5)
Glasgow Art Gallery and
Museum

VIII   The Widow's Visit   1899
La veuve en visite
Oil on paper on board
$19\frac{3}{4} \times 24\frac{3}{4}$ (50 × 63)
Art Gallery of Ontario,
Toronto

IX   At the Opéra   *c.* 1900
A l'Opéra
Oil on panel
$10\frac{1}{2} \times 8\frac{1}{2}$ (26·5 × 21·5)
Private collection, London

X   Child in a Room   *c.* 1900
Enfant dans une chambre
Oil on cardboard
$17\frac{1}{4} \times 22\frac{3}{4}$ (38 × 53·8)
The Art Institute of Chicago
(Mr and Mrs Martin A.
Ryerson collection)

XI   The Painter Ker-Xavier
Roussel and his Daughter
c. 1904
Le peintre Ker-Xavier Roussel
et sa fille
Oil on cardboard

23 × 21 (57 × 52)
Albright-Knox Art Gallery,
Buffalo, N.Y.

XII   The Café Wepler   *c.* 1905
Le Café Wepler
Oil on canvas
$24\frac{1}{2} \times 40\frac{5}{8}$ (62 × 102)
The Cleveland Museum of Art,
Gift of Hanna Fund

XIII   Marthe Mellot: the Garden
Gate   1910
Marthe Mellot: la porte du
jardin
Oil on canvas
$55\frac{1}{2} \times 74\frac{1}{2}$ (141 × 189·5)
Mr and Mrs Maxwell
Cummings, Montreal

XIV   Annette on the Beach at
Villerville   1910–11
Annette sur la plage à Villerville
A la colle on paper on canvas
$67\frac{3}{4} \times 48\frac{3}{4}$ (172 × 124)
Private collection, Paris

XV   Interior with a Lady and a Dog 1910
Intérieur (La princesse Gaétani
de Bassiano caressant un fox-
terrier dans son salon)
Oil on cardboard
$23\frac{1}{4} \times 29$ (59 × 73·6)
Fitzwilliam Museum,
Cambridge, England

XVI   The Black Cups (Misia Sert
and her Niece)   1919–24
Les tasses noires (Misia Sert et
sa nièce)
A la colle on canvas
$55\frac{1}{8} \times 68\frac{7}{8}$ (140 × 175)
Private collection, Paris

XVII   Sketch for Portrait of Pierre
Bonnard   *c.* 1925
Esquisse pour le portrait de
Pierre Bonnard
A la colle on paper
$44\frac{7}{8} \times 56\frac{1}{4}$ (114 × 143)
Musée du Petit Palais, Paris

XVIII In the Park at Les Clayes
c. 1936
Dans le parc aux Clayes
A la colle on paper
61 × 53⅛ (155 × 135)
Private collection, Paris

1–102 ILLUSTRATED IN MONOCHROME
(pp. 141–216)

1   Still-life with Bottle and Carafe
c. 1888
Nature morte avec bouteille et
carafe
Oil on canvas
15½ × 12¼ (39·5 × 31)
Mrs Charles Goldman,
New York

2   Dinner Time   1889
L'heure du dîner
Oil on canvas
28¼ × 36⅜ (72 × 92·5)
The Museum of Modern Art,
New York
(Gift of Mr and Mrs Sam Salz
and an anonymous donor)

3   Self-portrait in a Straw Hat
c. 1890
Vuillard coiffé d'un canotier
Oil on canvas
13¾ × 12¼ (35 × 31)
Private collection, Paris

4   The Goose   1891
L'oie
Oil on cardboard
8⅝ × 10⅝ (22 × 27)
Private collection, Paris

5   Two Little Girls (Little Girls out
Walking)   1891
Deux fillettes (Fillettes se
promenant)
Oil on canvas
32½ × 25¾ (82·5 × 65·5)
Mrs Stachelberg, New York
Not in exhibition

6   Lugné-Poe   1891
Oil on panel
9½ × 10½ (24 × 26·5)
Mr Fletcher Steele, Pittsford, N.Y.
Toronto only

7   Self-portrait in a Straw Hat
c. 1892
Vuillard coiffé d'un canotier
Oil on canvas
14 × 11 (35·5 × 28)
Mr and Mrs Ralph F. Colin,
New York
Chicago only

8   Self-portrait   c. 1892
Autoportrait
Oil on canvas
16¼ × 13 (41·5 × 33)
Mr and Mrs Leigh B. Block,
Chicago

9   Self-portrait   c. 1892
Autoportrait
Oil on cardboard
14⅛ × 11¼ (36 × 28·5)
Mr and Mrs Sidney F. Brody,
Los Angeles

10 Woman Sweeping   c. 1892
Femme balayant
Oil on cardboard
18 × 19 (45·5 × 48)
Phillips Memorial Gallery,
Washington, D.C.
Toronto only

11 The Elegant Lady   c. 1892
L'élégante
Oil on cardboard
10¾ × 6¾ (27·5 × 17)
Private collection, Paris
Not illustrated

12 Symphony in Red   1893
Symphonie en rouge
Oil on cardboard
23 × 25¾ (58·5 × 65·5)
Mr and Mrs Ralph F. Colin,
New York
Not in exhibition

13 The Kitchen   1892
    La cuisine
    Oil on canvas
    $6\frac{3}{4} \times 13\frac{1}{4}$ (17 × 34)
    Yale University Art Gallery,
    New Haven, Conn.

14 Dressmaking   1892–95
    La couture
    Gouache on paper
    20 × 19 (51 × 48)
    Mr and Mrs Hans Popper,
    San Francisco

15–23 Coquelin *cadet*   1892
    Watercolour,
    all approx. 8 × 5 (20 × 13)
    Private collection, Paris
    Toronto only (7 subjects)

24 Classical Comedy I   *c.* 1892
    La comédie classique I
    Watercolour and gouache
    $7\frac{1}{8} \times 15\frac{3}{8}$ (18 × 39)
    Private collection, Paris

25 Classical Comedy II   *c.* 1892
    La comédie classique II
    Watercolour and gouache
    $5\frac{7}{8} \times 14\frac{1}{2}$ (15 × 37)
    Private collection, Paris

26 Jeanne Raunay in *Iphigénie*
    c. 1893
    Jeanne Raunay dans *Iphigénie*
    Oil on cardboard
    $22\frac{1}{2} \times 19\frac{3}{4}$ (57 × 50)
    Dr S. Raxlen, Montreux,
    Switzerland

27 Stage Scene (possibly from
    Maeterlinck's *Pelléas et Mélisande*)
    c. 1893
    Scène de théâtre
    Oil on cardboard
    $11\frac{3}{4} \times 19\frac{3}{4}$ (30 × 50)
    Richard L. Feigen & Co. and
    Stephen Hahn Gallery, New York

28 Picnic   *c.* 1898
    Pique-nique

Oil on canvas
$102\frac{1}{2} \times 98$ (260·5 × 249)
Los Angeles County Museum of
Art (Gift of Hans de Schulthess)

29 Married Life   *c.* 1894
    La vie conjugale
    Oil on cardboard
    20 × 22 (51 × 56)
    The Hon. A. G. Samuel, London

30 The Square   1894
    Le square
    A la colle on canvas
    83 × 62 (211 × 157·5)
    Mr and Mrs Sam Jaffe
    Not in exhibition

31 The Entrance   *c.* 1895
    Le portique
    A la colle on board
    $23\frac{1}{4} \times 14\frac{1}{2}$ (59 × 37)
    Marvin B. Gelber, Toronto

32 Mme Bonnard   *c.* 1895
    Oil on cardboard
    $16\frac{3}{4} \times 12\frac{1}{2}$ (42·5 × 32)
    Mr and Mrs Paul Mellon
    Not in exhibition

33 Woman Sewing   1895
    Femme cousant
    Oil on panel
    $12\frac{5}{8} \times 14\frac{5}{8}$ (32 × 37)
    Museum of Fine Arts, Boston
    (John T. Spaulding Fund)

34 The Proscenium at the Théâtre
    Antoine   *c.* 1895
    L'avant-scène au Théâtre Antoine
    Oil on cardboard
    $12\frac{1}{2} \times 19\frac{1}{2}$ (31·5 × 49·5)
    Stephen Hahn Gallery, New York

35 The Family at Luncheon   1896
    La famille au déjeuner
    Oil on canvas
    $12\frac{1}{2} \times 18$ (32 × 45·5)
    Mr and Mrs Ralph F. Colin,
    New York
    Chicago only

36　Woman in an Interior　*c.* 1895
Femme dans un intérieur
Oil on canvas
$16\frac{1}{8} \times 13$ (41×33)
Albert Loeb and Krugier Gallery,
New York

37　Woman Seated in a Garden
c. 1896
Femme assise dans un jardin
Oil on panel
$6\frac{3}{4} \times 6\frac{1}{4}$ (17×16)
The Hon. David Dugdale,
Yorkshire

38　The Manicure　*c.* 1896
Le manucure
Oil on canvas
$13\frac{1}{4} \times 11$ (34×28)
Southampton Art Gallery,
England

39　Misia at the Piano and Cipa
Listening　*c.* 1897
Misia au piano et Cipa écoutant
Oil on cardboard
$23\frac{5}{8} \times 19\frac{3}{4}$ (60×50)
Staatliche Kunsthalle, Karlsruhe
Not in exhibition

40　In the Garden　*c.* 1895–98
Au jardin
Oil on cardboard on canvas
19×25 ($48\cdot5 \times 63\cdot5$)
E. V. Thaw & Co., Inc.,
New York

41　Luncheon at Villeneuve-sur-
Yonne (Misia with her Brother
Cipa Godebski)　1897
Le déjeuner à Villeneuve-sur-
Yonne (Misia avec son frère Cipa
Godebski)
Oil on cardboard
21×9 ($53\cdot5 \times 23$)
Private collection, London

42　Misia in the Fields　*c.* 1898
Misia aux champs
Oil on cardboard
$21\frac{1}{4} \times 26\frac{3}{8}$ (54×67)

Private collection, Paris
Not in exhibition

43　The Attic Room　1897
La mansarde
Oil on cardboard
$18 \times 25\frac{3}{4}$ ($45\cdot5 \times 65\cdot5$)
Mr and Mrs H. Wendell Cherry,
Kentucky

44　The Family in the Garden　1898
La famille au jardin
Oil on cardboard
$10\frac{5}{8} \times 43\frac{3}{4}$ (27×111)
Staatsgalerie, Stuttgart

45　Vuillard's Bedroom　*c.* 1898
Chambre de Vuillard
Pastel on paper
$12 \times 9\frac{3}{4}$ ($30\cdot5 \times 25$)
Mr and Mrs Hans Popper,
San Francisco

46　May Belfort　*c.* 1898
Oil on cardboard
$12\frac{1}{4} \times 19\frac{3}{4}$ (31×50)
Mr and Mrs Irving Mitchell Felt,
New York

47　Vuillard's Mother in Profile
c. 1898
La mère de Vuillard en profil
Oil on cardboard
$13 \times 14\frac{7}{8}$ (33×38)
John Hay Whitney collection,
New York

48　Interior with Mother and Child
1899–1900
Mère et enfant dans un intérieur
Oil on cradled panel
$16\frac{3}{4} \times 13\frac{3}{4}$ ($42\cdot5 \times 35$)
Mrs Philip N. Lilienthal,
California

49　At the Window　*c.* 1900
A la fenêtre
Oil on canvas
$24\frac{1}{2} \times 19\frac{1}{4}$ (62×49)
Mrs Wellington Henderson,
Hillsborough, Calif.

50 Window on Lac Léman   1900
Fenêtre sur le Lac Léman
Oil on cardboard
$24\frac{3}{8} \times 19\frac{1}{4}$ (62×49)
Dr Walter Feilchenfeldt, Zürich

51 The Red Roof   1900
Le toit rouge
Oil on cardboard
$20 \times 16\frac{3}{8}$ ($51 \times 41 \cdot 5$)
Tate Gallery, London

52 Downhill View Towards a
Garden   c. 1900
Vue plongeante sur un jardin
Oil on cardboard
$15 \times 10\frac{5}{8}$ (38×27)
Samuel J. Wagstaff Jr, Detroit,
Mich.

53 Félix Vallotton   c. 1900
A la colle on cardboard
$25\frac{5}{8} \times 19\frac{3}{4}$ ($65 \times 50 \cdot 5$)
Musée National d'Art Moderne,
Paris

54 Women in an Interior   c. 1900
Femmes dans un intérieur
Oil on cardboard
$22\frac{1}{2} \times 24$ (57×61)
Museum of Art, Carnegie
Institute, Pittsburgh, Pa.
(Presented through the generosity
of Mrs Alan J. Scaife Jr)

55 Interior   1900
Intérieur
Oil on paper on panel
$18\frac{1}{2} \times 25$ ($47 \times 63 \cdot 5$)
Private collection, Chicago
Not illustrated

56 The Family in the Drawing-
room at La Montagne, L'Etang-
la-Ville   c. 1902
La famille dans le salon de la
Montagne, à l'Etang-la-Ville
A la colle on paper on canvas
$26 \times 42\frac{1}{8}$ (66×107)
Private collection, Paris

57 Self-portrait   1903
Autoportrait
Oil on cardboard
$16\frac{1}{8} \times 13\frac{1}{8}$ ($41 \times 33 \cdot 5$)
Mr and Mrs Donald S. Stralem,
New York

58 Interior   c. 1904
Intérieur
Oil on panel
14×19 ($35 \cdot 5 \times 48 \cdot 5$)
Harry M. Goldblatt, New York

59 At the Seashore (Lucie Hessel by
the Sea)   c. 1904
Au bord de la mer (Lucie Hessel
devant la mer)
Oil on panel
$8\frac{1}{2} \times 8\frac{1}{2}$ ($21 \cdot 5 \times 21 \cdot 5$)
Dr Armand Hammer,
Los Angeles

60 The Bedroom   c. 1905
La chambre
Oil on canvas
$23\frac{5}{8} \times 26$ (60×66)
Kunsthaus, Zürich

61 Interior with Seated Woman
1904–05
Femme assise dans un intérieur
Oil on canvas
$17\frac{3}{8} \times 15$ (44×38)
The Art Institute of Chicago
(Charles H. and Mary F. S.
Worcester collection)

62 Child Lying on a Rug
c. 1905
Enfant couché sur un tapis
Oil on cardboard
$14\frac{5}{8} \times 20\frac{3}{4}$ ($37 \times 52 \cdot 5$)
Mrs John Wintersteen, Villanova, Pa.

63 Mme Hessel in her Salon at
Saint-Jacut   1905
Mme Hessel dans son salon à
Saint-Jacut
Oil on cardboard
$17 \times 20\frac{1}{4}$ ($43 \times 51 \cdot 5$)
Dr Peter Nathan, Zürich

64 Mme Hessel 1905
Oil on cardboard
$41\frac{1}{2} \times 30\frac{3}{4}$ (105·5 × 78)
Joseph Pulitzer Jr, Saint Louis, Mo.
Chicago only

65 View from the Artist's Studio,
rue de la Pompe *c.* 1905
Vue de la fenêtre de l'atelier,
rue de la Pompe
Gouache on paper, mounted on
fabric
$28 \times 61\frac{7}{8}$ (71 × 157)
Milwaukee Art Center collection
(Gift of Mrs Harry Lynde
Bradley)

66 Girl with a Doll 1906
L'enfant à la poupée
Oil on canvas
$19 \times 23\frac{3}{4}$ (48·5 × 60·5)
Mrs L. Monroe Glass, New York

67, 68 Studies for 'Place Vintimille' (p. 48)
c. 1906
A la colle on paper on canvas
each $76\frac{1}{2} \times 26\frac{1}{2}$ (195 × 68)
Private collection, Paris

69 Rue Lepic, Paris *c.* 1908
A la colle on paper
$65 \times 18\frac{1}{2}$ (165 × 47)
Dr Armand Hammer,
Los Angeles

70 Place Vintimille *c.* 1908
A la colle on cardboard
$39\frac{3}{8} \times 27\frac{1}{2}$ (100 × 70)
Private collection, Paris
Not in exhibition

71 The Art Dealers (The Brothers
Bernheim) *c.* 1908
Les marchands de tableaux (Les
frères Bernheim)
(Study for painting completed
c. 1912)
Oil on canvas
$28\frac{3}{4} \times 26$ (73 × 66)
City Art Museum of Saint Louis,
Mo.

72 Mme Hessel reclining on a Sofa
c. 1909
Mme Hessel sur un canapé
Oil on composition board
$14\frac{3}{4} \times 32$ (37·5 × 81)
Private collection, San Francisco

73 Breton Coast, Pouliguen
Lighthouse *c.* 1908
Côte de Bretagne, la phare de
Pouliguen
A la colle on paper
$21 \times 62\frac{1}{4}$ (53·5 × 158)
Mr and Mrs John David Eaton,
Toronto

74 The Saltings *c.* 1910
Les marais salants
Oil on cardboard
$19\frac{3}{4} \times 28\frac{3}{4}$ (50 × 73)
Albert Loeb and Krugier Gallery,
New York

75 Interior: Woman on a Sofa
c. 1910
Intérieur: femme sur un canapé
Oil on cardboard on cradled panel
$29 \times 34\frac{1}{2}$ (73·5 × 87·5)
Bristol City Art Gallery, England

76 View on the Binnenalster,
Hamburg *c.* 1913
Vue sur la Binnenalster à
Hambourg
A la colle on cardboard
$29\frac{1}{8} \times 21\frac{5}{8}$ (74 × 55)
Hamburger Kunsthalle

77 Dr Viau Operating *c.* 1914
Le Dr Viau opérant
A la colle on canvas
$42\frac{1}{2} \times 54\frac{3}{8}$ (108 × 138)
Musée National d'Art Moderne,
Paris

78 Mme Vuillard and Annette (In
the Drawing-room) 1915–16
Mme Vuillard et Annette (Au
salon)
Oil on cardboard
$29\frac{1}{2} \times 20\frac{1}{4}$ (75 × 51·5)

Musée Cantonal des Beaux-Arts,
Lausanne

79 The Drawing-room, rue de
Calais *c.* 1918
Le Salon, rue de Calais
A la colle on cardboard
26 × 28¾ (66 × 73)
Private collection, Paris
Not in exhibition

80 The Salle des Cariatides at the
Louvre *c.* 1918
La salle des Cariatides au Louvre
A la colle on canvas
59 × 65 (150 × 165)
Ian Woodner, New York

81 Study for 'The Salle des
Cariatides at the Louvre' *c.* 1918
Pencil drawing
Ian Woodner, New York

82 The Salle des Cariatides at the
Louvre (detail) *c.* 1918

83 Annette Dreaming *c.* 1918
Annette rêveuse
A la colle on paper on canvas
29⅛ × 27½ (74 × 70)
Private collection, Paris
Not in exhibition

84 Study for 'Mme Val Synave'
1920
Drawing

85 Mme Val Synave 1920
A la colle on canvas
44⅛ × 34¼ (112 × 87)
Private collection, Paris

86 The Sunny Room (Mme
Vuillard's room at Vaucresson)
c. 1920
La chambre ensoleillée (La
chambre de Mme Vuillard à
Vaucresson)
Oil on canvas
18¼ × 21 (46·5 × 53·5)
Minneapolis Institute of Arts

(Bequest of Putnam Dana
McMillan, 1961)

87 Dr Vaquez at the Hôpital
Saint-Antoine *c.* 1921
Le Dr Vaquez à l'Hôpital
Saint-Antoine
A la colle on canvas
55⅛ × 51⅝ (140 × 131)
Académie Nationale de Médecine,
Paris
Not in exhibition

88 Vuillard Washing his Hands
c. 1921–25
Vuillard se lavant les mains
Oil on cardboard
32 × 25 (81·5 × 63·5)
Ian Woodner, New York

89 Mme Vuillard Lighting her Stove
c. 1924
Mme Vuillard allumant son
fourneau
Oil on cardboard
26¾ × 28⅜ (68 × 72)
Norton Simon collection
Not in exhibition

90 Mme Hessel 1924
Oil on canvas
35½ × 24¾ (90 × 63)
Private collection, Paris
Not in exhibition

91 Mme Gillou at Home 1931
Mme Gillou chez elle
Oil on canvas
28½ × 36¼ (72·5 × 92)
Knoedler & Co., Inc., New York

92–98 Seven studies for 'Anna de
Noailles' *c.* 1932
Drawings
Private collection, Paris

99 Study for 'Anna de Noailles'
c. 1932
A la colle on canvas
43¼ × 49¾ (110 × 126)
Private collection, Paris

100   Anna de Noailles   *c.* 1932
A la colle on canvas
$43\frac{1}{4} \times 49\frac{3}{4}$ (110×126)
Private collection, Paris

101   Woman in Interior   1932
Femme dans un intérieur
Pastel and gouache on paper
$49\frac{1}{4} \times 37\frac{1}{4}$ ($125 \times 94 \cdot 5$)
The Art Institute of Chicago
(Gift of Mrs George L. Simmonds)

102   Interior with a Lady Sewing
c. 1935
Intérieur avec couseuse
Oil on canvas
$51\frac{3}{4} \times 38\frac{1}{4}$ ($131 \cdot 5 \times 97$)
Los Angeles County Museum of
Art (Gift of Mr and Mrs
David E. Bright)

Graphic Works

in exhibition

103–115 LITHOGRAPHS: ILLUSTRATED
(pp. 217–220)

103   Cover to 'Landscapes and
Interiors' series   1899
Couverture: 'Paysages et
intérieurs'
CRM 31 $20 \times 15\frac{3}{4}$ (51×40)
Private collection, Paris

104   Cake for Tea   1899
La pâtisserie
CRM 41 $14 \times 10\frac{5}{8}$ ($35 \cdot 5 \times 27$)
Private collection, Paris

105   On the Pont de l'Europe   1899
Sur le pont de l'Europe
CRM 40 $12\frac{1}{4} \times 13\frac{3}{4}$ (31×35)
Private collection, Paris

106   Pink Interior III   1899
Intérieur aux tentures roses III
CRM 38 $13\frac{3}{8} \times 10\frac{5}{8}$ (34×27)
Private collection, Paris

107   Interior with Hanging Lamp
1899
Intérieur à la suspension
CRM 35 $13\frac{3}{4} \times 11$ (35×28)
Private collection, Paris

108   Pink Interior I   1899
Intérieur aux tentures roses I
CRM 36 $13\frac{3}{8} \times 10\frac{5}{8}$ (34×27)
Private collection, Paris

109   Pink Interior II   1899
Intérieur aux tentures roses II
CRM 37 $13\frac{3}{8} \times 10\frac{5}{8}$ (34×27)
Private collection, Paris

110   The Fireplace   1899
L'âtre
CRM 39 $9\frac{1}{2} \times 10\frac{3}{4}$ ($24 \times 27 \cdot 5$)
Private collection, Paris

111   The Cook   1899
La cuisinière
CRM 42 $13\frac{3}{4} \times 11$ (35×28)
Private collection, Paris

112   The Game of Checkers   1899
La partie de dames
CRM 32 $13\frac{3}{8} \times 10\frac{1}{2}$ ($34 \times 26 \cdot 5$)
Private collection, Paris

113   The Two Sisters-in-law (Misia
Natanson and Marthe Mellot)
1899
Les deux belles-sœurs (Misia
Natanson et Marthe Mellot)
CRM 43 14×11 ($35 \cdot 5 \times 28$)
Private collection, Paris

114   Across the Fields   1899
A travers champs
CRM 34 $10\frac{1}{4} \times 13\frac{3}{4}$ (26×35)
Private collection, Paris

115   The Avenue   1899
L'avenue
CRM 33 $12\frac{1}{4} \times 16\frac{1}{8}$ (31×41)
Private collection, Paris

116–129 LITHOGRAPHS: ILLUSTRATED
(pp. 25–65)

116   Programme for the Théâtre
Libre   1890
$7\frac{1}{2} \times 6\frac{1}{2}$ ($19 \times 16 \cdot 5$)
Private collection, London
Illustrated on p. 25

130 Old Woman in the Kitchen 1893
Vieille femme au fourneau
CRM I 10 × 7$\frac{7}{8}$ (25·5 × 20)
Private collection, Paris

131 The Siesta, or Convalescence
1893
La sieste, ou la convalescence
CRM 2 11 × 8$\frac{1}{4}$ (28 × 21)
Private collection, Paris

132 Frontispiece: *Les Nouvelles
passionnées* (Maurice Beaubourg)
1893
CRM 3 7$\frac{1}{4}$ × 2$\frac{3}{4}$ (18·5 × 7)
Private collection, Paris

133 Interior 1893
Intérieur
CRM 4 7$\frac{1}{2}$ × 4$\frac{3}{4}$ (19 × 12)
Private collection, Paris

134 The Sleeping Child (The
Dressmakers) 1893
L'enfant couchée (Les
couturières)
CRM 5 8$\frac{1}{8}$ × 5$\frac{1}{8}$ (22 × 13)
Private collection, Paris

135 Folding the Linen 1893
Le pliage du linge
CRM 6 9 × 12$\frac{1}{8}$ (24 × 32)
Private collection, Paris

136 Interior with Five Poses *c.* 1893
L'intérieur aux cinq poses
CRM 7 9$\frac{1}{2}$ × 11$\frac{5}{8}$ (24 × 29·5)
Private collection, Paris

137 Interior with Screen *c.* 1893
L'intérieur au paravent
CRM 8 9$\frac{7}{8}$ × 12$\frac{1}{4}$ (25 × 31)
Private collection, Paris

138 Intimacy *c.* 1895
L'intimité
CRM 10 10$\frac{1}{4}$ × 7$\frac{1}{2}$ (26 × 19)
Private collection, Paris

139 The Studio *c.* 1895
L'atelier
CRM 11 9$\frac{5}{8}$ × 11$\frac{3}{4}$ (24·5 × 30)
Private collection, Paris

140 The Table with the Big
Lampshade *c.* 1895
La table au grand abat-jour
CRM 12 5$\frac{1}{2}$ × 8$\frac{1}{4}$ (14 × 21)
Private collection, Paris

141 The Dressmaker 1895
La couturière
CRM 13 10$\frac{1}{4}$ × 6$\frac{1}{4}$ (26 × 16)
Private collection, Paris

142 The Studio with Two Windows
c. 1895
L'atelier aux deux fenêtres
CRM 14 9 × 11$\frac{3}{8}$ (23 × 29)
Private collection, Paris

143 Luncheon *c.* 1895
Le déjeuner
CRM 15 9$\frac{7}{8}$ × 6$\frac{1}{4}$ (25 × 16)
Private collection, Paris

144 The Tuileries 1895
Les Tuileries
CRM 27 9$\frac{1}{2}$ × 10$\frac{7}{8}$ (24 × 27·5)

145 The Garden of the Tuileries
1896
Le jardin des Tuileries
CRM 28 11 × 17 (28 × 43)
Private collection, Paris

146 Children Playing 1897
Jeux d'enfants
CRM 29 11 × 17 (28 × 43)
Private collection, Paris

147 Motherhood 1896
Maternité
CRM 30 7$\frac{1}{2}$ × 8$\frac{7}{8}$ (19 × 22·5)
Private collection, Paris

148 The Garden in Front of the
Studio 1901
Le jardin devant l'atelier
CRM 45 24$\frac{3}{4}$ × 18$\frac{7}{8}$ (63 × 48)
Private collection, Paris

149 Project for Album Cover
   c. 1899
   *Projet de couverture pour un
   album d'estampes*
   CRM 47 $23\frac{1}{4} \times 17\frac{3}{4}$ (59 × 45)
   Private collection, Paris

150 In the Gallery at the Théâtre
   du Gymnase 1900
   Une galerie au Gymnase
   CRM 48 $9\frac{7}{8} \times 7\frac{1}{2}$ (25 × 19)
   Private collection, Paris

151 Poster for the Apéritif 'Bécane'
   c. 1894
   Bécane (affiche)
   CRM 49 $31\frac{1}{2} \times 23\frac{7}{8}$ (80 × 60·5)
   Private collection, Paris

152 Lucien Fabre 1924
   CRM 52 $5\frac{1}{8} \times 3\frac{1}{8}$ (13 × 8)
   Private collection, Paris

153 Tristan Bernard *c.* 1924
   CRM 53 $4\frac{3}{4} \times 3\frac{1}{2}$ (12 × 9)
   Private collection, Paris

154 Frontispiece: *La Cuisine*
   (Henry-Jean Laroche) 1935
   CRM 54 $12\frac{1}{4} \times 9$ (31 × 23)
   Private collection, Paris

155 The Menu (Jacques Laroche
   and Mme Hessel) 1935
   *Le menu (Jacques Laroche et
   Mme Hessel)*
   From *La Cuisine*
   CRM 55 $9\frac{7}{8} \times 8\frac{5}{8}$ (25 × 22)
   Private collection, Paris

156 The Butler 1935
   Le maître d'hôtel
   From *La Cuisine*
   CRM 56 $11\frac{1}{4} \times 8$ (28·5 × 21)
   Private collection, Paris

157 The Cook 1935
   La cuisinière
   From *La Cuisine*
   CRM 57 $12\frac{1}{4} \times 9$ (31 × 23)
   Private collection, Paris

158 At the Touch of a Match 1935
   La flambée
   From *La Cuisine*
   CRM 58 $12\frac{1}{4} \times 9$ (31 × 23)
   Private collection, Paris

159 At Table 1935
   Le repas
   From *La Cuisine*
   CRM 59 $12\frac{1}{4} \times 9\frac{5}{8}$ (31 × 24·5)
   Private collection, Paris

160–164 ETCHINGS: NOT ILLUSTRATED

160 Théo van Rysselberghe *c.* 1898
   CRM 61 $4 \times 5\frac{1}{2}$ (10 × 14)
   The Museum of Modern Art,
   New York

161 Interior with Sofa (Evening) *c.* 1930
   Intérieur au canapé (Soir)
   CRM 62 $4 \times 5\frac{7}{8}$ (10 × 15)
   The Museum of Modern Art,
   New York

162 Square Vintimille 1937
   CRM 64 $8\frac{1}{2} \times 6\frac{1}{4}$ (21·5 × 16)
   The Museum of Modern Art,
   New York

163 Little Studies in the Public
   Garden 1937
   Petites études dans le square
   CRM 65 $5\frac{3}{4} \times 4$ (14·5 × 10)
   The Museum of Modern Art,
   New York

164 Square Vintimille 1937
   CRM 66 $13\frac{1}{4} \times 10$ (33·5 × 25·5)
   The Museum of Modern Art,
   New York

Drawings
in exhibition

165–178 ILLUSTRATED (pp. 11–71)

165 Self-portrait drawing
   Autoportrait, dessin
   Private collection, Boston
   Illustrated on p. 11

166 Jacques Salomon at the Louvre
   Jacques Salomon au Louvre
   Private collection, Paris
   Illustrated on p. 15